# OF COURSE YOU CAN SING!

## By Michelle Cohen

Updated and Revised, Second Edition

# COPYRIGHT © 2005, 2014

♫

# DISCLAIMER

♫

# DEDICATION

This book is dedicated to you. Yes, you. Thank you for being someone who wishes to express yourself. You decided at some point in your life, that making music, being creative, using your voice and nurturing your talents, gifts and abilities was a worthwhile endeavor.

I applaud you.

# PREFACE

I have been on an incredible artistic journey. Through my ability to sing and to touch others with my talent, I have been handed great joy. This book is my chance to give you your opportunity to soar.

I grew up singing every single day of my life and getting paid to do so from very early on. I started at the ripe old age of six as Dorothy in *The Wizard of Oz* and have been having a blast ever since.

I have performed in over fifty musicals and plays, soloed in hundreds of concerts and was even given the honor of performing "Boy from New York City" for then Governor of New York, Mario Cuomo. I also began recording children's albums as a kid. I continued working in the studio into adulthood.

At first it was pure instinct and a gift that I enjoyed. Then I began studying seriously and discovered the craft. I also trained as an actress both in the U. S. (graduating from Sarah Lawrence College) and in London (The British American Drama Academy).

I got my Equity card right out of college. I toured in a musical revue of Broadway shows in Germany (it seems I got there right after a little known performer named Jennifer Lopez finished her leg of the tour!). In the show, I played such diverse roles as Maria in *West Side Story* (singing "Tonight"), Eponine in *Les Miserables* (singing "On My Own"), Christine in *Phantom of the Opera* (singing "All I Ask of You") and Grizabella in *Cats* (singing "Memory").

Immediately following that gig, I toured in *Nunsense* with Georgia Engel. Once I landed in New York City, I began performing my own cabaret shows. These include a wider variety of song selections - from jazz, pop rock, standards, classical to musical theatre. I started working behind the scenes as well, directing, producing and writing.

I had the great pleasure to be the New York Producer and General Manager of *Schoolhouse Rock Live!* (an adaptation of the ABC Emmy-Award winning cartoon). It was a hit and we ran the show Off-Broadway for a year before opening it up to national tours and regional productions. Now every state in the country can boast of some incarnation of the show at their local schools and/or theatres.

I am CEO and President of my own entertainment company which creates and produces innovative products in publishing, film, and television. (A whole other world that you can read about on my website at www.michellecohenprojects.com).

But most significantly for this book, I have had a private vocal coaching practice for over fifteen years and have taught at several acting schools including NYU. Also, as a director and producer, I have been on the opposite end of the spectrum, discovering how to optimize auditions, rehearsals and performances from that perspective.

Why did I start teaching? I was already busy, busy, busy with several projects at once. But numerous audience members began approaching me after performances asking if I would teach them how to sing. I always demurred, saying I didn't have the time. The truth was it just never occurred to me to examine what I did in order to assist others to do it as well. Eventually enough people were asking me that I started to wonder. What exactly was it that made everyone so happy and excited to hear me perform?

Then I started using Julia Cameron's book The *Artist's Way* with a very diverse group. It is a lovely tool for discovering lost parts of your creativity or redefining what you want to do and be in your life. I was amazed when every single person spoke with great longing for the ability to sing, to sing more, to sing better.

I was even more astounded by how many of them felt that they couldn't do it. I was suddenly struck with a question. Is it true? Can only some people sing and others cannot? I have to admit, when I started teaching, I wasn't sure

My practice built very quickly. I started with small groups, moved into private coaching sessions and eventually added performing arts schools from young performers to graduate level drama students.

And now, I can safely say, without any hesitation, after working with students from age eight to eighty. From Broadway performers to Christmas carolers. From the supposedly tone deaf to the actually blind. From the folk singing guitarist to the Marilyn Monroe impersonator. From people who want to learn a wedding song for that special occasion to the ones who want to sing karaoke well, just once in their lives...

Of course they can sing!

I have discovered that the running joke that everyone secretly wishes to be a rock star may not be off track. So whether you are actually working on a professional singing career or just want to have a better time in the shower, there are very specific things you can do in order to develop your sound, style and overall vocal production.

The first thing I remind my students is this: Madonna, Pavarotti, Bob Dylan, Wynonna Judd, Bernadette Peters, Jay-Z, Eric Clapton, Alicia Keyes, and Prince all can write SINGER on their passport. There are so many singers, so many sounds, and so many voices. Why can't you be one of them, too?

Well, you can. You just need the passport to your voice.

It is my pleasure to assist you. Enjoy!

# Contents

# WHAT THIS BOOK CAN DO FOR YOU

This book is rich with tricks of the trade, personal anecdotes and suggestions gathered over the course of a lifetime. The chapters are broken up into the following sections:

**SO MANY SINGERS, SOUNDS AND VOICES**
*listen – discover new genres – live music - pleasure, profit or both?*

**MEET THE INSTRUMENT - YOUR BODY**
*body awareness - relaxation - presence - gestures - eyes - clothes - breathing - breath-ing in or breathing out*

**MEET THE INSTRUMENT - YOUR SOUND**
*where is the sound in your body? - vocal range and break - belting and mixing -tone - listening to yourself - your mouth - vowels - consonants - diction - which direction to sing - pitch - tone-deaf - what key am I in? - vocal gymnastics - dynamics - money notes - mimicking*

**EXPRESS YOURSELF**
*lyric interpretation - getting the words into your mouth - emotional expression - visu-alization & sense memory*

**AUDITIONING**
*auditions - your call back bag - outfit - headshot - bio/résumé - the music - owning the room*

**PERFORMING**
*karaoke - group singing - singing back-up or duets - performing on stage - pre-show prep - to mic or not to mic - recording studios - sound and lights check - getting your footing on stage - long runs - bowing*

**OVERCOMING OBSTACLES**
*vocal health - nerves - who told you, you can't? - unfair comparisons - sing better? or stardom?*

**NOW WHAT?**
*the right teacher for you - instincts*

My tastes and abilities in singing are quite varied, so expect me to cater to many styles of music. This book is in no way a replacement for training. It is something you can use to get started, to get refreshed, or to get inspired. It is most importantly a guide to show what you are capable of and gently shoving...I mean supporting you in the direction of greater vocal fun.

# SO MANY SINGERS, SOUNDS AND VOICES

**LISTEN**

First and foremost, you need to listen to music. To singers. To anyone and anything you can lay your hands on. CDs, concerts, television specials, movies, old recordings, the latest radio releases, whatever band, show or musical event is happening in your town. You may do this already. But now you get to do it with an eye (and an ear) towards your own musicality.

Start listening not just for your pleasure, but also for your abilities. When you notice someone doing something you like, try it yourself! Did someone just wail on the National Anthem? Go into your room and see how it feels to do the same thing. You may be terrible! But at least you have tried on some new notes for size. That's awesome! Think of it as a shopping spree. You have a free pass to every mall in the country, and you get to decide what fits and what you are taking home with you. And whatever feels too tight or just doesn't look as good as it did on the hanger... leave it in the dressing room without a second thought. You may surprise yourself and discover something you never knew you could do before! But most importantly, you are trying on everything

**DISCOVER NEW GENRES**

Make sure you also experiment with music you think you hate. We tend to get into listening ruts and need to shake things up a little. I did not "get" country music for a really long time. Until I realized I never actually attempted to sing it myself. So, in the privacy of my own room, I decided to go for it. I turned the radio to a never before dialed station and went to town. Lo and behold! It's fun. Way sexier and vocally interesting to sing then I expected. And when I took the time to really listen to many of the lyrics, they were terrific and some of them even hysterical! On the other hand, while I know I have the lung capacity and the ability to sing opera, to the end of my days, it is just not a type of singing that I enjoy. But I can appreciate what those hardworking musicians are capable of, now that I have tried it.

The great thing about expanding your musical horizons is that you will begin to notice more details. You will become able to break down the mechanics in a much more enlightened way. Including discovering aspects of singing that are universal whether you are Billie Holiday or Billy Joel. Then you can notice the fascinating ways they apply these abilities in such vastly different songs

## MUSICAL STYLES

*Blues - Hip-Hop - R & B - Broadway - Jazz - Rock & Pop - Choral - Metal - Rock & Roll - Classical - Modern/Alternative Rock - Soul - Country - Opera - Specialty (from atonal to yodeling) - Folk -Pop - Funk - Reggae — World*

## LIVE MUSIC

Growing up in New York gave me the unique opportunity of going to Broadway, Carnegie Hall, Madison Square Garden, every year, numerous times a year. But you don't have to live in an entertainment metropolis to find new sounds. What's playing in your hometown? And have you checked out music from your local library lately? I go all the time and make sure I hit a section I normally would never look. This way I can hear new music but not have to invest in it if it ends up not being my cup of tea.

I have had the great fortune to observe and hear live some of the most compelling singers of our lifetime. And still, after every performance, I go home and start playing with what I noticed while I was there: Another way to hold the microphone, a radical approach to hitting a note, an entirely different interpretation of a song I have been singing for years. I see these performers not as competition but as mentors. Learn from the best!

So, once you have narrowed down the huge possibilities of musical genres into the "I love this stuff " or to the "never again will this pass my lips," now it's time to figure out what you are good at.

Why?

Because you need to decide something else as well…

## PLEASURE, PROFIT OR BOTH?

What do you sing for pleasure? And what do you sing for profit?

You may love to sing standards, but your gritty sound is more suited to the blues. That's cool. Sing standards for fun. Learn the blues for the public. This kind of self-awareness will save you from heartache later. I can't tell you how many people have auditioned for me through the years, sure that they sounded like what I was asking for in the audition notice, only to be dumbfounded when gently let go. You see it all the time on the initial *American Idol* preliminaries. People who have not listened with a discerning ear to their own voice.

So instead of letting themselves shine, they simply sing what they like and are not brilliant at it. At all.

Again, you may have no desire to be a professional. But just imagine going to the next family gathering and shocking everyone with your beautiful rendition of "Happy Birthday" instead of the "too high for you, cracking on the final notes" version everyone has come to expect. Just by knowing what sounds you make best, will have an amazing effect on you and the reception to your singing.

# MEET THE INSTRUMENT – YOUR BODY

## BODY AWARENESS

So the first thing any musician must do is obtain their instrument. Lucky you! There is no fee involved. But the smart musician will inspect, test, and become intimately acquainted with their instrument. As a singer, that means introducing yourself to your body and your voice in a completely new way.

The best way to start is with a deep breath. Great. Take another. Now here's the fun part. The next time you take a breath, imagine breathing into your back. Cool, huh? We tend to forget that we are three-dimensional beings. Since our literal focus through our eyes is forward, we tend to function through our day with a flat sense of our bodies. It is imperative to feel all of the support you can by adding attention to the back half of your body as well as the front.

The more you become aware of your body, the more it will work for you. You may be standing in such a way that stops the flow of breath or you may be holding your body in a position that makes it very hard to sing higher notes. Start to pay attention to yourself as you go about your day. Notice when you hunch, when you stretch and where you stiffen up.

# EXPERIMENT

*Experiment with routine habits: stand at a different angle in the shower, brush your teeth with your other hand, walk at a much slower pace and then speed up and back again. You will start to notice all kinds of shifts in your body and where you habitually place tension.*

*The reason to do this is that you want to optimize how you align your body so that you can produce your best sound. Sometimes it is as simple as fixing your posture that makes all the difference in the world. Are you leaning slightly forward onto your toes or backwards onto your heels? See if you can center your balance in the middle of your feet. By redistributing your weight, you can literally redistribute your sound.*

## TRICK

*If you are feeling awkward in how you are standing, place one foot slightly in front of the other. This tends to help situate you in space and looks great to the audience as well. Don't be afraid to stand at a slight angle as opposed to straight out to an audience. This gives you more freedom to move side to side and will feel more normal.*

Are your knees locked as you stand and sing? Let them bend slightly and note how much better that feels. This is a big habit breaker for many people. It may feel like there is more control by locking the knees but it actually makes you more rigid and less fluid. Think of the Tai Chi Masters who are always bending and shifting their legs. They are ENORMOUSLY powerful.

More classically trained singers are taught to keep their shoulders back in order to open up the chest. Exaggerate hunching over and then rolling your shoulders back to get the gist of the difference. Keeping your shoulders back also gives an air of confidence and openness that serves any singer well.

It is very important to keep the neck lengthened and the head floating easily on the top of the spine. Since your larynx and vocal chords are housed in your neck, you want to give it as much room to give you the best sound. I sometimes find it hard to figure out how to align my neck and head properly since you need to contort yourself to see it in the mirror.

## EXERCISE

*A great exercise for loosening up those neck muscles and spine is as follows:*

*Lie down on the floor (don't use your bed for this one, you need a harder surface, but a mat is fine). As slowly as you can imagine, let your head rotate to the right as far as it can go. Then even slower, let it rotate all the way to the left. Keep breathing as you do this and allow for all the time in the world.*

*We put the heaviest weight (our heads) onto our little necks. They could really use attention and relief. When you have brought your head back over to the right, let your entire body curl up on the right side and slowly work your way to standing. Let your head wobble*

*Of Course You Can Sing!*

*gently as you go and when you are finally erect, it will feel looser. Imagine your head as a balloon floating up to the sky. This will lengthen your neck and as you relax back to a normal pose, your head will be in much better alignment with your spine*

## RELAXATION

Exploring relaxation techniques are as vital to life as they are to singing. In our goal-oriented society, relaxation has become a luxury instead of a necessity. It is up to each individual to claim his or her right to live in ease, in fluidity and in bliss. So I strongly recommend any version of relaxation that works for you, be it meditation, visualization, yoga, dancing, swimming, etc. And try to make that a more constant part of your life routine.

In fact, singing should be one of those things that become a relaxing element in your life! Here's how to move into that...

The first step towards relaxing is noticing that you're not relaxed! We tend to go, go, go and then collapse at the last possible moment. Not the best way to get a more grounded and secure performance out of yourself. This will always lead to vocal fatigue, and sometimes to out of control sounds being produced because you are too tired to handle the song.

The more you can release your muscles and gain mobility, the freer your sound will become. And the looser you are, the more sounds you can produce. And when you are relaxed, you are better able to command your body and control what you want to sing.

So, let's notice which parts of your body feel limber. And which parts are tense? Is the tension something you have been living with forever? Or are there new aches and stiffness? Really explore how your body holds its stress.

Now start to breathe. Breathe into any part of you that could use some help easing up. Breathe as if you are making a wish on your birthday candle. You know, the huge intake of breath and then the steady flow out to make sure you get them all in one try! (But don't get tense breathing!!!!) Wish your overworked muscles a better year. By sending that message, the body part will automatically release itself.

While you're at it, start recognizing the parts of the body

Michelle Cohen

we tend to ignore. Breathe into the back of your thighs. Breathe into your heels. Breathe into your butt. Imagine tension melting away from your elbows. Introduce yourself to the obscure parts of your body that are just craving your attention. When was the last time you breathed into your earlobes?

It may sound silly. But truly, your body registers when you are giving it your full attention especially to the slightest details. You may be amazed at the response. This will help not only the sound you make but also any nerves you might have. They tend to melt away when you breathe from such a steady place. This gives you a solid sense of grounding.

I find this a great exercise to do in bed before going to sleep. It is soothing, it is interesting, and it's a great way to slow my mind down and fall into a delicious sleep. (By the way, if you get dizzy or if anything doesn't feel right, please be wise and stop immediately. I am in no way a believer in "no pain, no gain.")

So now that you have done a detailed accounting of your body, bring your attention back to the initial request. Take a deep breath, but now breathe into your back and your front at the same time. Feels completely different doesn't it?

**PRESENCE**

There is another important aspect about you as an instrument that I highly recommend implementing. Since your body produces the sound and it is what people are looking at when you are performing, it is imperative that you feel great about being inside it. And that does not mean making a single external adjustment. I really mean, as long as you are aware of your body's gifts and your body is clear that you are thrilled to be in it, the audience will sense that instinctively.

As a culture, we tend to spend way too much time judging and criticizing ourselves and not enough time giving love and thanks for the remarkable machine that keeps us going every day. So even on those days when you can't imagine why you should get out of bed, be kind to this miraculous engine that keeps working no matter what you say to it. Even if all you can think to do is thank your pancreas for secreting so well, think something positive and watch your body respond in kind. Also, the nice thing about being a singer is that there is no measurement you must meet, there are no height requirements, and it really doesn't affect your vocal range if you are having a bad hair day.

Remember, Beyonce, Meatloaf, Edith Piaf, Mama Cass, Luther Vandross and Cher could not look less like each other. But all of them project great stage presence. Every physical type has the ability to be seen in its fullest glory. So do not for a moment think that yours cannot as well. It is merely a question of you believing in your right to perform, to be heard and to be seen. It is more important to commit to what you are doing than to be preoccupied with how you are looking. My mom told me about her experience many years ago at a Chekhov production at Lincoln Center that I have since heard repeated by others who were lucky enough to be there at the time. It seems the woman playing the maid was somehow more compelling than the leads (played by the estimable Irene Worth and Raul Julia). No one could take his or her eyes off of this young woman. Why? She was Meryl Streep. Check out the varied looks she has in each of her movies. This simply proves, it's what is burning inside her that counts, not what color her hair is.

I recommend discovering the pleasure of living inside your skin so that when you stand confidently and present yourself, everyone sees a million dollar product!

**GESTURES**

So, in case you haven't noticed, we haven't made a single sound yet. Pretty weird for a singing book, huh? Not really. I think it is imperative to get a sense of your surroundings and feel incredibly comfortable before beginning.

Part of getting situated with your body, is starting to notice your habits. Do your hands move a lot when you sing? Do you balance awkwardly on one leg when standing? Does your body sway? Does your neck strain upwards when going for the high notes?

Most people, when they really get into the music, fail to notice how their body is responding.

Again, in the aspects of singing that are for pure pleasure, this is not a big deal. But if you are planning on having people watch you, it's something to consider. Some people have signature movements; Mick Jagger's chicken walk, Judy Garland's arm wrapped against her chest, Jessica Simpson's hand gesticulating. So if there is something you love and feel great about, by all means keep it. Just know that you are doing it and make it a choice.

There is nothing more unnerving than hearing a friend comment, "Oh, you know that head thing you do all the time" and have no idea to what they are referring!

So, observe yourself. Go through a song and instead of thinking about the music or the lyrics; notice what your body is doing. You'll sense pretty quickly which way your limbs or torso want to go. And then you can decide what to keep and what to retrain.

Also notice if you tend to get stiff when singing.

A great exercise is to move around the room while you are working on a song. It gets the blood flowing and loosens you up. I always start my warm ups with vigorous shaking of my hands and feet and then my entire body. It wakes me up and gets the adrenaline flowing to a closer approximation of how I will feel when I am finally on stage.

## FUN TRICKS OF THE TRADE

*If you feel awkward just standing still, with your arms at your side, place your middle finger against your thumb. It gives the hand a sense of connection.*

*If your hands seem to want to move of their own accord, assign them specific words that they are allowed to punctuate. This will calm them down a bit during the rest of the song.*

*If your upper body tends to sway uncontrollably, add some swaying to your hips. That will equalize the energy and makes for a sexier presentation.*

Everyone has interesting facial gestures when they sing. Sometimes ya' just can't be pretty and hit that note at the same time. However, do notice if you seem to use your eyebrows a lot. This is not usually the best way to produce sound and most of the time indicates tension instead of emotion. We will talk more later about using the face to help produce sound, but for the purposes of this chapter, just notice when you are scrunching in pain, or your eyes are bugging out in panic. Both looks are probably not your best, and could be replaced by a more serene countenance. Make sure your forehead and eyebrows are expressing what you intend. You want to have the audience looking surprised and pleased that you can sing, not you.

While you are focusing on the face, it's also a great place to experiment with signature expressions. Where would Billy Idol be without his snarl? Is your smile incredibly charming? Feel what makes your face light up as you shine your talent on the world.

You can also do this work visually with a mirror, a video camera, or a REALLY FRIENDLY friend. However, I must put out a word of kindness and caution. It takes awhile to get used to seeing yourself from the audience's perspective. Think of how you feel when you get photos back from a trip. It sometimes takes a moment to register that this is what you look like. Now add movement and expression to that. It is very daunting to be brave enough to look at yourself in order to understand what could be made better. It takes at least three viewings before you can even start being objective. So be very careful of your psyche when you first begin watching. And if you find you cannot do it without being overly critical and mean to yourself, stop immediately. Nothing is worth that.

**EYES**

There is always the question of singing with eyes closed or open? I think it depends on the song and the venue. If you are singing a duet on stage, it's probably wise to keep your eyes open as you are supposedly communicating to the person next to you. Then again, if you are alone and revealing a very intimate moment, it is sometimes more interesting to watch the performer go deeply inside themselves to reveal what is there. The only thing I would advise is to make sure you are not closing your eyes in order to hide. There is something so beautiful about really connecting visually with the audience. If that is too frightening, it might be something to look at (literally and figuratively).

The ability to express emotion through our eyes is one of our greatest performance gifts. There is nothing worse than watching a performer (I see it all the time in auditions) literally stare as if they are deer in the headlights. It is a very immediate way to evaluate whether someone really wants to be there or not. Next time you watch your favorite performers, notice their eyes. There is nothing more compelling than the warmth that emanates out of Josh Groban's or the sparkle in Shania Twain's. Your eyes are always telling us how much you want to be there as well as the emotions you are conveying. Use them well.

As for crying when performing, it really depends on your ability to hang on until the end, or whether holding tears back will cause you to suffer vocally. If you are moved at some point and feel the tears trickling, by all means allow for it. Just try not to be a mess throughout an entire song. It tends to make the audience more uncomfortable for the performer and takes them out of the performance. You want them relating to the pain that is being put forth, not concerned for your personal wellbeing.

If you are performing a song that has a huge impact on you I strongly recommend working on the song on your own in many ways. Try it full out emotionally, just so you know how it feels to let go. And then try it without letting the emotion have its final release. Keep experimenting so that you are prepared. This way whatever happens in performance will not debilitate you. I am usually offered major tearjerker songs in shows. The worst experience is to suddenly have the emotional resonance of the song take over so that I am no longer able to finish the piece. I have learned to let that happen in rehearsals where I can excuse myself and become a puddle, instead of in front of thousands of people on stage.

## CLOTHES

I recommend wearing them. Unless you are in a production of *Hair*.

What to put on this body of yours while you are singing? Here's my favorite part: Anything you want! Unless you are playing a specific role or working with a costume designer, clothes and beauty are truly in the eyes of the beholder and wearer. It might be smart to make sure that you can breathe well (19th century corsets do put a cramp in breathing properly). But the best part about being a singer is that you can discover your signature style of voice and clothe it with your signature style of

*Of Course You Can Sing!*

fashion.

Do keep in mind that when you choose to wear something that is more revealing, or extra specially tight, your voice will now be vying for attention with whatever part of your body you are currently exposing. There is nothing wrong with that. Just know it and work with it. In fact, it is a GREAT attention grabber in the right situations.

Just try to make sure that your outfit is congruent with what you are presenting. I see countless women audition for the role of the young ingénue looking like they are ready to go out clubbing. While I appreciate being able to get a sense of what their body looks like, it is strange watching people sing the sweet, missionary Sarah Brown's songs from *Guys and Dolls* while dressed to play the dancehall hottie, Adelaide.

If you really want all attention to be on the voice and not your body, dress accordingly. That is why most choirs traditionally wear robes, or black and white. It is not about the individual physicality of the performer, it is simply about the sound.

## BREATHING

The most important aspect to singing is not the body or the voice. It's the breath. The more you work on developing your breathing apparatus and using it optimally, the better singer you will become.

When you take a breath, it is quite probable that your upper body moves up as you use your lungs and chest. Well, that's a start. The problem is, real breathing commences lower down. Much lower down. It includes your belly. And the more expert you become, breathing should include your navel as well. Some singers swear by breathing and singing from, shall we say delicately, their nether regions.

# TRY THIS

*Take this opportunity to place one hand on your chest and the other on your stomach, just above your belly button. Try to let your chest extend forward instead of up. Many people raise their shoulders as well when breathing. Try to keep them down and relaxed. As you take a breath in, see if you can feel both of your hands move out instead of up.*

*Great! Now your ribcage is engaged. When you feel comfortable with both hands moving together, switch the lower hand to below your belly button. See if you can push out that hand while you breathe as well. This is engaging your diaphragm. Super!*

Do note, many people are resistant to expanding their bellies because they spend a lot of energy sucking in their stomachs. Now is not the time to worry about flat abs and the perfect figure. Now is the time to be proud of the flexibility your body has and allow it to reign freely. I promise you, you will not get fat by breathing correctly. Actually it will probably have the opposite effect, since more breath assists the blood's circulation and metabolism!

Another big reason people only breathe from the neck up or from the chest up, is it keeps their feelings in check. Think about it. When you are experiencing deep emotions and expressing them (crying, yelling in anger, laughing), it tends to emanate from your gut. What's the best way to keep from feeling? Well, most people literally stop breathing from any place lower than their chest, and they tense their shoulders and their neck...All of the things we are trying to relax in order to sing better. So do know that to breathe from any lower in your torso, automatically connects you to your emotions.

This is a great thing for an artist. A direct link to what you are feeling. But it takes courage to choose to break through that barrier we put up in regular life and see what is deep inside.

Watch people throughout your day and notice how deeply or shallowly they are breathing. I sometimes find myself taking deeper breaths just to compensate for someone else's tight breathing.

Once your diaphragm is actively engaged, your vocal power is endless. It is situated quite literally in the middle of your body. So it gives a wonderful centering from which great sound can come. It also builds up your capacity to hold notes longer and to come at them with a strength that just can't be fulfilled with shallow breathing.

After you have grasped the concept of deeper breathing, the next level is adding in the back of you. Just as I asked you originally to notice breathing into your back, it's a great opportunity to literally place reserve breath there. So place your hand on your lower back and see if you can push it out on the exhale. Do this for your sides and waist, as well. It is remarkable where you can take breath from once you are open to looking for it.

## BREATHING IN OR BREATHING OUT

There are many schools of thought about the best way to breathe while singing. Some are literally opposite, so experiment and see what works better for you.

The more common technique is to intake a deep breath, filling your lungs, your diaphragm and letting your belly expand. Then as you let the notes come out, your belly contracts, pushing the air though the diaphragm, up past the chest, picking up the sound in the vocal chords and letting the music ride on the breath out through the mouth.

I had a teacher in college who gave me a glimpse into another option that was truly fascinating. Thomas Young is an extraordinarily gifted singer (even though he has jaw dropping credits, I got a kick out of the fact that he also happened to be the singing voice for Mighty Mouse). I was lucky enough to study with him while at Sarah Lawrence College. He suggested an approach, which to this day still gets me excited whenever I use it. You use the same intake of breath as described above. But when it is time to sing, instead of contracting the belly as you exhale, you continue to expand the belly outward as far as it can go. (You always have more breath than you think you do, so this is not farfetched in the least).

It may take a couple of tries to get the hang of it especially if you are well trained in the other manner. But play with it. I have found that keeping the belly inflated while exhaling brings an extreme amount of power into your midsection that builds in intensity instead of deflates. This gives the ability to create a grounded and fluid sound that is harder to maintain when singing the other way, so it's well worth the effort!

Also, I discovered an interesting challenge when working with dancers. I produced and directed an original ballet in New York City and some of the dancers came to me for vocal coaching. What we recognized really quickly was that dancers are trained to hold themselves up and to hold their stomachs in. This can lead to confusion when trying to find the best way to breathe as a singer. Just know this when you work with a teacher and make sure that you work together to find the best way to breathe, sing and dance in harmony.

Once you have chosen your favorite way to breathe, it is recommended that you work to stretch your capacity. The more air you have to work with in any given song, the more you can do. It's really fun to be able to choose to hold a note for an extended amount of time as opposed to gasping for breath after every measure. A fun way to practice is to pick a song and see how far into it you can last on one breath. This way you can mark your progress as you become able to sing further into a song than you did last week. The main purpose is to always be able to choose when you need a breath in a song, instead of your weaker muscles choosing for you. Try to have some breath left over when you come to your next breath. It is way too exhausting to have to gasp for help too many times within a song, and that stress will register pretty quickly.

When working on a song, there are several aspects of breath of which to be aware. First of all, as soon as the introduction to a song begins, start inhaling. It can happen slowly if the intro is long. What you don't want is to take a quick gulp and jump in at the last second. It does not prepare you and is a perfect giveaway to not being a pro. It also helps steady any nerves you might have about opening your mouth and letting sound come out.

Something else to think about are quick catch breaths. Sometimes the tempo is so fast, or the words are so tricky that there is no time to do a deep inhalation. So, practicing finding a quick moment to breathe is very useful.

There is also the use and misuse of breathiness. The sign of breathiness is when more air than sound comes out. This can be used with great seductivity as in Marilyn Monroe singing "I Want Be Loved By You." As always, make sure it's a choice. If you find yourself singing a breathy rendition of "We Will Rock You," you are probably not finding the right balance between air and sound.

*Of Course You Can Sing!*

# MEET THE INSTRUMENT: YOUR SOUND

## WHERE IS THE SOUND IN YOUR BODY?

What? Did you hear right? We are actually going to make noise? No more heavy breathing? Really?

OK, wise guys, here we go.

The first thing is making sure you do not sing from your throat. Even though your vocal chords are situated there, that is the last place where you want to be singing from. On your exhalation, the breath will be passing through the throat, picking up the notes from the vocal chords and then traveling to other parts of the body to resonate out. You should never try to push the sound from the throat area. I find that one of the stranger aspects of how our body works. But you are sure to get into vocal trouble, sore throats, sore chords or even worse, nodes, if you allow music to emanate from your throat.

If you need to, imagine breath is a date coming to pick up the sound from the vocal chords, but not wanting to hang out at the home with the parents still in it. So the breath and sound get out of there as quickly as possible.

Or whatever image works for you.

So where do you direct the sounds then? Basically, from your chest, face, and head. These are categorized into registers: the chest voice, the middle voice, and the head voice (falsetto for men).

Let's explore the chest register first. This is the lower part of your range. It can sound gritty and gravelly or deep and resonant. It should feel all rattley in the chest. To find that sound, start tapping your chest while saying "AHHH." Make sure the sound is not in your throat but actually coming from your chest. Now start to let your voice climb up the scale. Notice when the vibrations start to hit your jaw and mouth. You have now left the land of the chest. Slide the notes back down as low as they can go. Keep the sound below the throat. Congratulations, you have discovered your notes if you ever want to sing "Ole Man River" or "The Blues In The Night."

Now for something completely different. The head voice.

This is the top part of your range. It is really important that you don't strain to get up there. Again, stay away from the throat. The best way in is to imagine you are an owl. Cooing very lightly "WHOO" as if from the top of your head. You should feel vibration in your forehead and up around the top of your scalp. Kind of tingly. The less you think about it the higher you can probably go. If you get into Mariah Carey territory, consider yourself very impressive. That takes absolute relaxation and daring to perch so high on the scale.

The chest and the head voice are the two extremes of your vocal range. Most of the notes you will be singing sit right in between, in the middle register. When you pick up the sound and it begins to move through the mouth, imagine it hitting the upper palate and ricocheting out the upper lip, nose, cheeks and forehead. That's your usual target for most ranges.

Singers generally term this part of their face, the mask. It's sometimes useful to actually imagine that you are wearing a mask in order to better direct the vibration. It gets all tingly and buzzy when it's working correctly.

Great singers know where to place a note in their mask for optimal effect. So the more you practice and discover how yours works, the better your singing will become. Ultimately you want most of your face vibrating with sound when you sing, that's how you know it's working well.

I find chewing and scrunching my face a very valuable warm up before I sing anything. Getting my muscles limbered up and ready to resonate is akin to setting up your speakers for optimal stereophonic sound.

## VOCAL RANGE AND BREAK

In school chorus, you were probably labeled a soprano, alto, tenor, baritone or bass. This could be where you have a strength or tendency to sing, but it does not in any way limit you to that range and that range only. So I will not be utilizing those terms since everyone I have ever worked with has shown me they were capable of more octaves than they were usually given credit for. (With all due respect to the more formal singers in the bunch who must work within these regulations, disregard this next sentence or two). If you were labeled with a specific range as a child, I highly recommend you throw out any categorization. Discover for yourself just how high or low you can go. I know people who were placed in the alto section simply because they could hold harmonies really well, only to discover later in life they were actually incredibly gifted sopranos!

Now here's the tricky part. No matter what your vocal range, you have this. It is the dreaded word for every singer. It's called "the break." I don't know of anyone who is not intimately acquainted with his or hers. It is the part of the voice that has a tendency to crack just when you REALLY don't want it to. Most singing technique is centered on how to negotiate the breaks in one's voice so that they become part of the team instead of an obstacle. It's not hard to find. Just go up and down the scale a few times. Wherever your voice catches and you switch into a distinctly different sound, that's where your break is. Not a big deal once you know how to work around it. Most people like to train with me because mine is pretty much undetectable and they want to know how I figured out how to do that.

One thing to do is remain very aware when you are about to jump from one part of your voice to the next. And prepare for it. If you are singing in your chest voice and need to leap up into the top part of your range, start to lighten up on the effort you are using. The higher you get, the lighter you should be singing in order for those higher tones to soar. So a couple of notes prior to the jump, start adjusting the sound. This will give your voice a chance to navigate the break with less pressure and more certainty that the sound you want to make is what will occur.

Here's something else I have learned. The more forward you keep your sound, literally laying against the mask and pouring out of it, the more likely you can bypass the break. It's when we try to produce sound in the middle of our throat or from the back of our head that we get into trouble.

## TRY THIS

*Let your voice glide up and down as if you were a siren, using 'OOO' to accompany the scale. Now try to make the sound from the middle of your body, placed literally in line with your spine and back. You probably find at least two breaking points. Now try it again and place the sound up against your mask. Imagine the vibration falling against the front of your body, nowhere near your center. I bet it was much easier! And the break was far less noticeable.*

An interesting phenomenon to keep in mind. You will need to listen more than feel the results. For some reason, you can sound like you have negotiated around your break easily but it will feel like a huge mountain you barely leapt over. Trust you ear and other people's reactions despite what you are sensing from inside your body.

## BELTING AND MIXING

Another voice option includes belting or mixing. Different people have different interpretations of what they are and how they are done. Many people warn against excessive belting. What they are actually warning you about is the placement of the sound. If you are screaming or wailing from your throat, yes, indeed you are going to get into some serious vocal trouble. However, if you learn the proper way to literally mix your sounds, you can have a very healthy singing career.

What you are doing when you are mixing is literally joining registers together. The traditional belt of Ethel Merman was when she took her chest register and added it to her middle register as high as it could go. You can see in music created around the time of her stardom, the highest notes to belt were usually somewhere around C or D. That is because there is no way that I am familiar with to bring your chest register up even higher and still be singing in a healthy manner.

Today's mix/belt has a very different approach. It brings in the head voice. I have a theory on how and when that came to pass, which I am happy to share. Up until Barbra Streisand emerged in the 60s, most people were singing more distinctly in chest or head voices. You were either Rosemary Clooney or Doris Day. If they were mixing at all, it came from the chest up (as in the Ethel Merman example). Then along came Ms. Streisand who was suddenly mixing her sound throughout her range. What she is actually doing is taking her soprano and bringing it down to her middle register instead of bringing her chest up. Anyone who has done as many musicals as I have will note the HUGE difference between singing the songs in Rogers and Hammerstein scores

*Of Course You Can Sing!*

vs. the songs of Andrew Lloyd Webber. The only similarities *Oklahoma* and *Evita* share are their one-name titles. Nowadays, Broadway musicals like *Rent* or *Wicked* can have women belting as high as F and G with no problem. And in the pop world, I bet even Bing Crosby would have had to make some adjustments to handle some of the notes Mark Anthony hits.

What today's mixers and belters are also doing is singing in their higher registers, but they are not lightening up on the sound. This is why it is important to understand how to direct the notes into your mask. Most excellent mixes vibrate intensely in the nose and cheek area. Again, what they are doing is bringing the sound down from the head and forward into the mask. It leads to many more colors and much more options of range.

If you listen to early Celine Dion before she became world famous (I think just anything prior to *Beauty and the Beast*), you will notice the latest phenomenon to hit the pop world. Her mix used to be richer because she used her nose and her cheeks, spreading the sound around her upper face. But in order to get higher and higher, she needed to narrow the focus into her nose only and right between her eyes. It's a reedier sound but it gives just enough room to get those stratospheric notes without resorting to a more legit soprano sound.

**TONE**

Ultimately what distinguishes singers from each other the most is their tone. That is what the music sounds like coming out of you. Is it lilting and pure? Is it trumpeting and loud? Is it breathy? Is it nasal? There is usually a type of quality that your voice has in general. And then there are aspects that you can adjust depending on the attention you give.

If you find you are falling into a breathy category or a pinched tight sounding category, you should probably examine how you are connecting your sound and your breath. A breathy sound is literally too much breath and not enough music. If you are coming across pinched, you probably do not have enough breath to support the notes you are trying to sing.

Many people have an issue with nasality. This is a great gift when trying to do mix belting but may not serve a sweeter song.

This is usually caused by too much concentration in the center of the nose, and not enough vibration happening around the nose, in the cheeks, lips and forehead. Imagine spreading your sound to your ears and see how your music warms up.

Taste in tone is absolutely up to the individual. The richness or the coolness is as varied as there are instruments in an orchestra. Do you prefer violin or tuba? Are you like a reed instrument or a harp? Feel free to play with different textures and allow your own sound of music to come through.

### LISTENING TO YOURSELF

Here's the other big adjustment in finding the ultimate performance vocals. Most people when they sing are enjoying the sound as much as their listeners. If they are, that means the sound is still inside, and they have not fully let it out. Remember, the point is to hit the mask, let it resonate and let the sound ooze out of the face directly to the audience. Your face is the speaker, not the headphones. You should be listening for your voice outside of your head. Letting your ears be in front of you. And what you should hear inside are the leftover echoes of the music. It sounds pretty hollow.

Most people get pretty bummed when I tell them this. I know I was when I discovered it. But I started experimenting. And hands down, every time I let the sound leave me, I absolutely floored the audience. My suggestion is to record yourself doing it both ways. It is sort of astounding to hear the difference. Now mind you, when I am just playing on my own, I will absolutely keep the sound in my head, for my own listening pleasure. But I have also trained myself to project very differently when I am preparing a song for the public.

I think it's great to record yourself and listen. I used to do it as a kid. I would set up my tape recorder next to me at the piano and listen to the playback for hours. It really helped me notice when I was producing a sound accurately and when I wasn't. It takes awhile to become objective. But especially if you want a recording career, it is important to have the ability to listen to a playback and not want to run screaming from the room.

## YOUR MOUTH

Let's get more intimately acquainted with your mouth. It handles many responsibilities for making your music.

Since breath and sound travel out through the mouth, it is imperative to give them as much space as possible. That is why singers spend a lot of time loosening their jaw and making sure it is dropped to make room. Be very conscientious as you move your jaw around. It is a place where many people hold A LOT of tension. If you don't want to say something or are hanging on to an emotion, the last possible place to hold back is right there. By clenching the muscles around the jaw line, no one can make you say something you don't want to say. So be very tender and loving toward that part of you. Gently move it up and down and around and encourage it to loosen up. My first voice teacher used to say, "drop your molars" which was another way to imagine keeping everything open.

You also want the back of your throat to be as wide as possible, the way it is when you yawn. Actually the more you yawn, the more relaxed you become. So make sure yawning is a major part of your warm up. It stretches the face, gets you breathing more deeply and makes great room for sound to come out. In order to sing with such a wide-open throat (hard to ultimately do if you are still yawning), imagine you are swallowing a basketball. You want your upper palate lifted as high as possible. Make sure there is tons of room so that your sound can come through unobstructed.

Don't forget your lips while you are loosening everything up. They are such vital aspects to enunciation and vibration. The more versatile they are, the more options you have to express your words. The best exercise is to blow air through them (like what horses do) and let them flap together. Babies do this all the time. They must be warming up for when they will be able to communicate!

Your tongue can sometimes hold tension. Try to keep it as loose as possible. It is incredibly useful especially for faster songs or tricky lyrics. You may want to do stretching exercises (the tip of the tongue against the back of your front teeth while the middle of the tongue falls over the front teeth.) When you are singing, check in once in awhile to make sure it is resting easily and out of the way when not in use.

And for those of you who are singing with others or are playing opposite another performer, PLEASE be kind and make sure your breath is fresh. I had a fellow actor who thought it was very funny to eat Doritos just before our romantic scenes, every night. No amount of mints or hints worked. Then I decided the only answer was to eat garlic AND onions before a show. He was minty fresh until we closed!

**VOWELS**

When you sing, the sound travels on the vowels, "A-E-I-O-U." And what I find fascinating is that the order of those vowels travel from the back of your mouth to the front. Start with "A" (which is actually two syllables, the last of which turns into an "E") so start the first syllable or "EHHH" sound. That is produced at the back of your throat. No matter how hard you try, an "EHHH" will not begin right behind your lips.

Now let's move to "E" pronounced like "EEEE.." That moves a little bit forward but still not past the middle of your mouth. It also begins to incorporate your upper palate and jaw motion in order to produce that sound.

"I" is the combination of "AHHH" and "EEEE" and moves those sounds to the center of the mouth. Isn't this cool?

"O" is again a combination of "OHHH" and "OOOO." But the sound tends to originate toward the front of the mouth and becomes "OOOO" simply by closing your lips. All of this is front mouth movement.

"U" is literally the "OOOO" sound generated by closing the lips on the "OHHH."

And when the "Y" is added at the beginning of that vowel, it utilizes the entire mouth mechanism from the back to the front.

Try each of the vowel sounds slowly. Really taste each sound and where it lands in your mouth. Just for fun, try it backwards as well. "U-O-I-E-A.." Excellent!

## CONSONANTS

Now onto the consonants. Notice that they are very hard to give sound to without the addition of a vowel. There are a couple of exceptions that work when you are humming like "M," "N," and "V." But for the most part, consonants are simply anchors for the sound that comes through on the vowel that follows.

Feel the difference when you simply say "OOOO." Now put an "M" in front of it. You probably had a stronger tone. Observe where your mouth, tongue and lips place themselves in order to produce these letters. They are a great source of stability. Use it. Also keep an eye out for the more explosive letters like "P" or "B." Especially when recording, you may want to soften your approach to these so as not to knock out the microphone.

I don't usually pick favorites, but if there were any letter in the English language that I could encourage you to make friends with it would be the letter "M." Humming is the best thing you can do with your vocal warm-ups and for your overall vocal health. Before ever thinking of opening your mouth in the morning. I recommend you hum a bit. It just helps wake everything up. It gets your mask to vibrate, your lips to tingle, your placement nice and forward and you start your day off on a great note. It's also a good way to get new songs into your voice without taxing it. There are days, if I am tired, I will do my warm-ups on a hum first. Just to help every part of me wake up and be prepared for when I ask it to do harder work later.

## DICTION

So now we have our vowels and our consonants. Let's turn them into words. I advise early on when you are learning a song to go through the entire piece strictly from a letter placement point of view. Let's use the title words from the Frank Sinatra tune "I Did It My Way."

First skip the consonants and simply sort through the vowel sounds. "Ah-ee, ih, ih, ah-ee, eh-ee". Repeat that a couple of times so that it really travels around your mouth. Then just try the consonants without the vowels. "D-D-T-M-W." Just hit them around until they feel really stable. Now string the consonants and the vowels slowly together in speech. Don't sing it yet. Just notice the linking of one word to the next. It should feel rather sing-songy already. Finally add the notes to this exercise. The words should come out crisp and clear. Congrats! You have officially created the passageway for the music to really bounce. The words will never feel less than precise in your mouth again!

When you are holding a note, keep singing on the vowel and only close out the word with the consonant at the very last moment. When finishing the National Anthem, keep singing the "A" part of "brave" instead of the "V" until you are complete.

For more pop oriented songs, enunciation is less important. Indeed, if you over emphasize certain letters, you can sound incredibly weird. So feel free to ease up on words in order to let the music come forth. However, be careful that you don't end up as a legend of confusion. Everyone I know has a lyric that they absolutely misheard and turned it into something else (usually hysterical). I love LeAnn Rhimes but I am still not sure if she doesn't want to live or leave without you. Just be aware that by giving up clear diction, you may be giving up clear understanding.

Also a note about tongue rings. Yes, it is possible to sing around them, but you usually have to rearrange many of your mouth mechanisms and put a whole new technique behind it. Just a surprise one of my students went through when she randomly decided to pierce her body. We worked through it, but it was an effort.

## WHICH DIRECTION TO SING

Now lets actually look at the production of the notes themselves. As I mentioned before, the main thing not to do is strain when you are singing. It should feel easy and effortless. The less tension, the more soaring the sound. So presuming you are breathing well, projecting your sound from your chest, mask and head while bypassing the chords, you are in good shape.

Something I teach is the way to approach the notes. So many singers when they ascend the scale literally look up in order to get there. That, to me, is akin to staring at Mount Everest while trying to get your footing at the bottom. It's pretty daunting to say the least!

My suggestion is no matter what the note you are about to

hit, imagine you are at the top of the mountain and looking down on the note. You should feel as if you are already above the highest note. In this way, as you go to hit it, you imagine it is somewhere in your middle range and that makes it an easy one to achieve. It's always easier to go down stairs than to go up them. I think it's the same with the mental imaging of singing down towards a note instead of striving up to it. I even will tilt my head forward and my chin down in order to nail certain notes.

So if you were to sing the main section of "Over The Rainbow," my guess is your first impulse would be to imagine the big old jump between "Some" and "where" as you are hitting the notes, and perhaps your neck and chin are inching up as well. It is entirely possible to sing this way. But if you want to KNOW you are going to hit those notes and hit them beautifully, I recommend by the time you sing 'Some' to already imagine yourself hanging out at the mountain peak. So that 'Some' is an easy low note and 'Where' is also coming from somewhere (pun intended) further down the slope as well. So you pull the notes up to you instead of push up to them. Then when you sing the rest of the phrase, it is easy to just play.

**PITCH**

There are many tonal ranges within each note. It is entirely possible to swim within a pitch. You may have heard of someone being too sharp or too flat. It isn't that they aren't singing the correct note; they are just hitting the outer limits of the pitch of that note.

Imagine a target used for darts. Everyone wants to hit the bulls eye. Many people come in to the left or right of it or hit it too high or too low. That is where "pitch problems" lay. Another reason to "come down" on a note (as I explain in the "which direction to sing" section) is it tends to correct pitch problems automatically.

In order to tell if you have a pitch problem (sometimes it just shows up in certain songs, or it can be a more constant issue), I recommend paying attention to your singing one note at a time. Just try a single note and notice if you are confident about how it is coming out, or whether you are tentative. Sometimes pitch issues are simply an overcautious resistance to just going for a note. The opposite can be true, too. An overzealous singer can also get very sloppy and overshoot their target. The point is to really practice each note and make sure that your voice is very comfortable. Also, that your brain is really clear what note comes next and how you are planning to hit it. If you can, tape record yourself and listen for when you might be getting flat or sharp. Be honest with yourself, it doesn't help to ignore these little issues, 'cuz boy can they get bigger later!

Another reason for pitch problems is the infamous switch from singing on your own, and then singing with accompaniment. It actually takes awareness to make this transition. Adding the other notes of music to your own can be distracting at first. Especially if you are suddenly singing with an orchestra. Don't panic if it takes a couple of tries to get used to singing well with arrangements. You may have had different sounds or beats in your head so it might take awhile to adjust.

If you learned your song from another artist's recording and are now trying it on your own, be very aware of possible changes. The keys may be different, or the arrangement completely other. Also many times, a singer's sound was 'sweetened' in the recording studio and it is physically impossible to actually achieve live what they are doing. You may also discover that you don't know the song as well as you thought you did if have been using the other singer to support you.

Be very conscious as you step out on your own as to what your voice wants to do. If it gets shy or nervous or unsure, then you can be pretty sure that it will not hit the notes exactly on target. Practice, practice, practice. Have friends, teachers or loved ones listen to confirm that you have those notes pitch perfect before presenting them.

The more you learn exactly where your sound should be coming from in your body, the more likely you are to sing the notes you are supposed to be singing. It is something that a natural singer takes for granted, but it is completely learnable for others.

## TRICK

*Another fun trick that has helped many singers is to hear the note in your head just prior to singing it. Literally imagine the note, sung perfectly and then actually do it. It's kind of like the sports stars who imagine hitting the perfect golf ball, or home run. Visualizing it and then making it happen.*

*I find this especially useful for a high note or one that you are unsure as to whether you can nail it or not. As you get closer to the measure, just hear it in your mind and let your voice match that. It's a lot of fun and works surprisingly well!*

Something else I would recommend for those singers who read music. Sometimes, just looking at certain notes or discovering what key something is in can cause tension. I think many times we are better off remaining in the dark about where we are in our range so that we can surprise ourselves. So many singers, once they decide, "uh-oh—that's my break", or "oh no, I can't hit anything higher than an E", will have no problem if they are not looking at the music. And then after singing through a few times, they go back to the piano and discover that indeed they hit a high G!!!

The other reason is sometimes the pages are used as a security blanket. It is so important to get those notes inside you and for you to get a really organized sense of how notes come out of you. To spend a lot of time staring at the music sometimes takes away the organic possibilities you might discover by just playing with the notes on your own for awhile.

## TONE-DEAF

I'd like to spend a moment on people who have gained a reputation for singing off-tune or being tone deaf. There are indeed some people who have a harder time finding their note. It has NEVER been my experience that they can't eventually find it. Many supposedly tone-deaf people are actually always singing a third higher or lower than the song is written. First check to see if that's the case.

I have noticed something with many students who were told they couldn't sing or had pitch problems. I found they simply had not learned proper placement of their sound. They did not understand where their voice should go in relationship to the note they were hearing. Practically every single one of them actually had HUGE ranges. They were simply never shown what to do with them. Someone who has the option of two octaves with which to sing but doesn't know it, many times picks the wrong one and ends up sounding not so good. Whenever I work with these students, helping them get situated within their own voice and where their sounds should be placed in their instruments, they end up correcting what had seemed like impossible tone-deafness.

Of all the people who have come to me having been told they couldn't sing, only one person in that entire time proved to be a huge challenge. But he persevered, determined to overcome whatever obstacles stood in his way. Instead of working on an entire song each week, we went slowly, measure by measure, studying the possible ways he was not hearing where he should be placing the sound and coming up with solutions. He would then go home and with his tape recorder, practice the section we had studied throughout the week. Most of his fellow students surpassed him, perfecting many songs that semester. But none of those students received the kind of excitement, awe and respect for his final presentation of the entire song he had worked on for months, bit by bit, in perfect tune and with tons of heart! So with the right amount of work and support around you, anything is possible!

**WHAT KEY AM I IN?**

It is not necessary to read music to be a singer. However, it is necessary to understand what key you are singing in and more importantly, what keys work for you. From this perspective, learning basic music theory or just how to pluck out scales on the piano, may serve you well. So either commit yourself to learning to be a musician as well as a singer, or else make good friends with musicians you can turn to for help.

Finding out your range is useful for a myriad of reasons. This way, you will be really clear, really quickly, what songs are written with you in mind and which ones would need to be adjusted for you to perform well. If something is written that includes a falsetto range, you need to know whether you have that ability or not. It is very easy to expand your range with practice. The more you do vocal warm-ups and the more you stretch your muscles, the more notes will begin appearing on both ends of your voice. But even as you are expanding your repertoire, it is important to keep in mind, which notes are already easy for you.

A great experiment is to take a song you love and sing it in several different keys. Do it really high, do it really low, do it in the middle. Notice how that affects the song and the sound. Then for a subtler experiment, just change half a tone. If you are singing in Ab, move it into G, then move it to A. Believe it or not, it really makes a difference. Notice how singers tend to sing in certain keys all the time. They have discovered which ones show off their voice the best, and they have music transposed to those keys.

If you are using sheet music for auditions or for performances, MAKE SURE IT IS WRITTEN IN THE KEY YOU WANT TO SING IT IN!!!!!! You are in for a terrible surprise, if the way you have been practicing is not how the piano player is playing. It is pretty easy nowadays to get music transposed. There are computer programs or go back to that musician friend you made in the above paragraph, and ask them to assist you. It can be as simple as changing the chords (especially if you are working with guitar accompaniment). But do not assume someone can transpose on sight. That is a highly specialized skill, and not everyone has it. Also, you want to have as much control over your environment as possible in order to ensure your great performance. This is something you can easily have control over—so use it!

A note about sheet music…Most music is NOT written in the key that the original artist sings it in. It has been rewritten to fit the needs of the publishers, not the singers. It might have been put in an easier key to play or an easier key to notate. So do not assume, just because you have your favorite artist's best hits music book that it is also in the key you have been singing along with on the recording for all those years!

## TRY THIS

*Something I recommend: once you know what keys you sound great in and are really comfortable there, make sure you stretch yourself and experiment in other keys. You may be wobbly at first, but you also may discover a different timbre you didn't realize was part of your voice. Hidden treasures are in each key. It's up to you to uncover them.*

## VOCAL GYMNASTICS

There are many options, aside from hitting a note directly each time. One of the most common, especially in popular music, is the scoop. That is literally working your way up into a note so that you hit it dead center at the very last moment. Sliding notes from either direction is also a very effective way to tease your listener before bringing home the tone. Old style crooners and blues singers are brilliant at using this effectively.

Then there is the latest trend of what I call "everything but the note." This is the kind of rolling around within the chord structure that has been popularized by people like Christina Aguilera. It's a lot of fun. And the more you can jump around and add new licks to the measure, the more impressive this becomes. I just add one cautionary plea…every once in awhile, actually hit the note! It is incredibly gratifying and will help set off the times when you don't.

Do make sure you have actually learned the song the way it was written first. It may surprise you to recognize that the composer spent a considerable amount of effort coming up with the note progressions. So at least honor their work by learning what they wanted before taking off into a totally different version of the song.

Also, consider whether the song you are singing merits the stylizations you are choosing to use. Sometimes it can be fun to reinvent a song. But a lot of times it just sounds inappropriate. A straightforward song like "Send in the Clowns" would sound pretty odd if done in an "Aretha Franklin at her most extraordinary" way. Doesn't mean you can't put your own imprint on the song, but just make sure your vocal choices don't overpower or disempower what the song asks for.

Another big part of singing is vibrato. Some people have it naturally, some learn it, some have too much, and some have too little. A lot of it is up to the individual singer and their taste. Just make sure it is something you are controlling instead of it controlling you. Many people find that their vibrato gets a bit unwieldy the more nervous they get. That is why it is imperative to have great breathing technique so that it doesn't get the best of you.

It should be your choice when you want to add that little tremor to a held note, or to a type of song that could use a delicious trill. To practice, just pick a note and sing "AHHH." Do it straight and plain, then slowly add some vibrato to it, making it more heavy, then lightening up. Keep doing this until it becomes second nature to you. If you find that your vibrato is not happening, you are probably putting too much pressure on your chords. Check your posture and any tension in your neck. Keep experimenting. It takes tremendous focus to rework your vibrato so do not get discouraged.

When you are deciding on the stylizations of your song, be they heavy on the gymnastics or really old school smooth, be really conscious of yourself as an instrument. In the same way a violinist can add fingering to make a note vibrate, you are capable of renegotiating a sound in so many different ways. Does the song require that you bleat like a trumpet? Is it so rhythmic that you consider yourself a percussive addition? Are the notes so important that you must sing them fluidly or can they be thrown away in favor of a shout, a groan or a scream? The voice has so many options; it's incredibly exciting to have all of these at your fingertips. Don't do yourself the disservice of treating every song as if it were the same. Color your music with all the colors of your vocal range.

Feel free to pepper certain songs with scatting, humming or various percussive sounds. Where would Jazz or R&B be without it? As always, learn from the greats…nothing like a little Ella Fitzgerald, or Ray Charles. So many new artists are adding such interesting musical interludes into their songs. Don't feel like you have to be a slave to tradition. Absolutely feel how the music is moving you and if new notes and configurations start flowing out of you, by all means make the song your own!

## DYNAMICS

The dynamics of a song are so important and so personal; they can really make or break a great presentation. The most obvious dynamics are simply loud versus soft. Deciding at which point you let a note rip and when you keep it quiet are exciting explorations of a song. It is sometimes harder to keep a note light than it is to punch it. It takes great breath control and strength to keep it steady and musical.

When choosing which way to go within a lyric, remember what reaction you will cause by your sound. Loud and impressive notes will literally (assuming they are done well and are not piercing or pitchy) lift the spirits and the bodies of your listeners. When you sing softer, you are inviting them into your spell. They tend to lean forward and work a little harder to hear you, which can sometimes be very effective.

Most people tend to begin their songs with a lighter touch, and then move into a more aggressive sound. This serves many purposes. It gives the song a chance to build, and the potential for shading and coloring. Many times, the chorus is the loudest section while the rest of the song is softer. This makes sense, the chorus is usually the point of the song, and you want to make sure to get it across.

There is also an opportunity to augment a note that is held longer. Don't always assume that you should start soft and get louder. Some of the more impressive and interesting endings to songs are when that final note is nailed strongly and then lightened up to release us from the moment.

Most importantly you want to build an arc to your song. You want to know where the climax is. Many times it is the highest notes in the song. Other times it is the section just before the ending, giving the singer a chance to add some final thoughts to what has just been revealed. It is important to decide for yourself where you think the climax is, and to make sure that the coloring you give the song leads you to it.

When I say coloring, what I am referring to is the different shades you can give a note. You can punch certain notes, use staccato, a sigh, a growl, syncopated rhythm… So many possibilities, so start creating a treasure chest to use as you work on a song and see which ones might fit the bill. Here is where being breathy, or doing a run (many notes surrounding the note you are actually aiming for) could be perfect! Sometimes doing what is normally looked upon as bad singing is exactly what is needed.

Another useful idea that I employ is not singing a certain note and speaking the word instead. This can be incredibly moving. It will bring extra attention to that lyric, so when it feels right, absolutely feel free to do it.

Remember, your voice is an instrument and as such, you are free to make whatever music you can think of that serves your pleasure and those of your audience.

Unless you are scatting or humming, you are singing words. Figure out what the language is calling for and what style it needs to be expressed. And that can be something that is unexpected, too. Some of the best songs are surprising reinterpretations of older ones. So see how the song speaks to you and in what way you want to impress your talents onto it.

## MONEY NOTES

Money notes are really fun and can literally lead to lots of cash if you become particularly talented at them. What are they? They are the big notes that set you apart from the rest of the crowd. The coloratura who can hit high C. Mariah Carey who can sing in octaves above high C. They are usually employed in the power ballads, think Journey's Steve Perry in "Open Arms" or Celine Dion's "All By Myself." It's the notes that everyone, whether they realize it or not, holds their breath to hear. You can build great anticipation of it coming and raise the excitement when you hit them so smoothly and remarkably. This invariably leads to immediate applause sometimes before you are even done.

And here's the thing, you may not have the range that these performers have, but if you discover what a harder note for your range is and you dramatically lead the audience to anticipate it and then you ace it, you have created your own version of a money note.

It basically comes in two categories. The truly amazing notes that not many people can deliver, and then the approach to a note that drives a crowd wild. Adam Duritz of Counting Crows is not trying to hit Placido Domingo's high notes but he sure as hell knows how to work that gravelly sound and make it thrilling.

So once you have discovered what your money notes

are, look for songs that cater to them. I happen to have an exceptionally high mix/belt, so I look at songs that Faith Hill or Linda Eder are singing because they are usually written in keys that cater to those higher money notes. If I am looking at Norah Jones, that will be awesome music but not high enough to show off my top sound.

I will put in one word of caution. Do try to show diversity. Don't try to hit your money notes in every single song you sing. Less is more. This is something just like in dynamics, you want to lead up to it and it needs to seem special. If you do it all the time, it becomes something predictable and almost humdrum. Michael Jackson's high pitch additions to his songs are done so much, that they are no longer money notes, but part of his regular expected sound.

Someone once pointed out something that Judy Garland did that has stuck in my mind forever more. She was a super singer and able to belt some really great money notes. She also gave the impression of great fragility which made it that much more incredible when she would overcome all obstacles and wow everyone with these phenomenally strong and heartfelt songs.

She was a workhorse though. And it was entirely possible that there was never a doubt in her talent that she could hit those notes. But part of the thrill for her as well as the audience was the possibility that she couldn't. It kept the danger and the suspense laced in her performances. Whether it was real or completely staged, it worked.

My point is, add drama to your money notes. I always know I am going to hit them. I have worked long and hard to have that kind of assurance in my voice. However, I will make it seem like its a bit more difficult or I am taking a risk. It's a funny game to me but it's a highly effective one. So play around and have a great time exciting yourself and the people you are performing for!

## MIMICKING

One of my first callbacks in New York City, right after graduating from college was for the long running off-Broadway hit, *Forbidden Broadway*. It is a wonderfully witty musical that pokes fun at whatever shows are currently on Broadway plus some of the more iconic legendary singers. Four consummate singers and mimics perform songs in the style of whomever they are spoofing.

I was asked for the call back to learn, among others; Barbra Streisand, Liza Minnelli, and Julie Andrews. It was an utterly fascinating exercise. I got music and videos of each of them and studied their physical gestures, facial expressions as well as how they were placing their sound in their bodies.

I discovered quite a few things that have helped me become a better singer than I ever was before (and also showed me that I am quite a good impressionist as well).

First of all, I saw that certain gestures were imperative in order to create the sounds they were making. Julie Andrews may look like she is impossibly happy anytime she sings. What she is actually doing is lifting the upper part of her face in order to assist with the beautiful soprano tone she lets out. I would never have discovered this if I were simply singing along with her. There is something infinitely incredible about actually trying a singer on for size! Get inside their bodies and really ape their gestures. Do them for real and then exaggerate them. You will be amazed!

I also discovered parts of their emotional life by mimicking their performances. I completely understand Liza Minnelli's over the top magnetism, having let my body pretend to inhabit it for awhile. Now again, I am not advocating becoming any of these people (unless you are preparing a drag show…). But now that I have tried on Liza, when I get to a certain point in a song and want to turn up the star quotient, I know whom to use for inspiration.

It is also the best way to learn performers' gifts. I was working on Barbra Streisand whom I had been singing with my entire life. When I actually tried to sing as her, I discovered something huge. She is a soprano! She takes her soprano range and brings it down instead of taking her chest voice and bringing it up. It is why she is at such ease in any register. I took this revelation and applied it to my own sound. Lo and behold, I could suddenly sing with much more force than I ever had up until that point. Pretty incredible!

A fun by-product to this exercise is you can be a smash at any party. Once people get a hint of your extracurricular abilities they will be clamoring for your Dolly Parton or Usher impressions. Especially if you've got the moves down as well as the voice!

After you have played with this opportunity, spend time pondering what makes you special.

What is unique to your sound or gestures that will cause people to want to do you in the future? The point of impressions is exactly that—you have made an impression. What is your signature?

Listen to singers you love. What makes them stand out for you? Is it the way they ease through a lyric like Tony Bennett or Sarah McLaughlin? Is it how they feel everyone's pain like Janis Joplin or Willie Nelson? Is it how they electrify when they take over the stage like Melissa Etheridge or Sting? Do they dance as well as sing like Ricky Martin or Britney Spears? Or do they wield their power behind an instrument like Lenny Kravitz or Tori Amos? All of these people have found their sound, their movement, their presence and their style. Note them and then find yours.

You can usually hear the influences that these singers grew up on as well. Where would KD Lang be without Roy Orbison? What would so many alternative female singers sound like without Joni Mitchell to emulate? What male rocker isn't paying homage in some way to Elvis Presley or James Brown? Listen to the greats in whatever genre of music interests you. They have tapped into something universal and long lasting. Discover what that is for you.

Oh, and in case you were wondering…I did not get the job at *Forbidden Broadway*. I was way too young for the gig at that time. Welcome to showbiz!

*Of Course You Can Sing!*

# EXPRESS YOURSELF

## LYRIC INTERPRETATION

Until now we were mostly concentrating on the sound, the notes, the production of music. In this section, we are going to explore the other half of what a song is: the words. This is where I have a very special affinity, since I grew up as an actress as well as a singer. I have brought my acting training into my music. Not just for songs that actually tell a story, but for any kind of lyric, even if it is simply scatting or nonsensical words like *Supercalifragalisticexpialidocious*! There are wonderful techniques to approach these words and I am dedicating this part of the book to them.

I suggest taking the lyrics and putting them on a separate sheet of paper so that you can look at them in paragraph form, away from the music. Read the words aloud as a story and start to see what they mean. What is the lyricist trying to say? What is the meaning behind these words?

One of my favorite quotes (and I wish I knew who said it) is that musical theatre is not larger than life; it is as large as life. Taking that out of the niche genre and placing it into the bigger picture of music as a whole...Why are we singing? Because what we have to say is so big, and so important, merely speaking is not enough. We have been handed the gift of the gods. We can transport others and ourselves to a higher plane in order to express everything we are thinking and feeling. Whew! No wonder we should take a little time and see what it is we are doing!!!

When you are looking at the song and its meaning, work on two parts. What does the song literally mean? Make sure you understand every word of the song, and if you don't, look it up! Then also look at what this song means to you. There must be a reason you picked it out of the gazillions of songs in the world. Why does it resonate for you? What do you have to say with this song? The more personal you make it, the more likely people will be thrilled to hear your unique voice!

If you are building up a repertoire of music, take a step back and look at the themes weaving through your choices. Are they all about love? Are they all serious and intense? You may decide to really push a theme that interests you or you may decide you have one too many songs about how your ex-boyfriend done you wrong. If that is the case, look for other ideas you might want to say with music. I have been blown away by the messages my inner creative self has been sending me when I look at the songs I am gravitating to at certain points in my life. It has helped me either mine the depths of an emotion I have really wanted to explore, or it has helped me get out of a stuck place I didn't even know I was in to then breathe life into new aspects of my life.

On the flip side, sometimes it is really fun to take a song and turn it on its ear. Add an ironic swing to a too saccharine song. Or put a funny spin on a serious subject matter. The more creative you let yourself get, the more people will be waiting to hear what new clever song you have in your treasure chest. Gwen Stefani took one of the most traditional songs steeped in one of the most traditional musicals "If I Were a Rich Man" from *Fiddler on the Roof* and made it hip and happening with her rendition of "Rich Girl." It's fantastic!

As you read through the lyrics, start to break them down into sections. Sometimes that is done for you with an intro, a chorus, a refrain. Look at words and lyrics that are repeated. Why does someone repeat himself or herself? Do they think they are not heard, that what they are saying isn't getting through? Or is it for themselves, they can't believe what they have discovered so they need to say it over and over again. Just really delve into the possibilities and try different versions. It is usually pretty obvious which one feels right for you.

When you feel you have gotten everything out of looking at the lyrics separately, go back to the sheet music and look at the words in the context of the music. Go slowly, measure for measure. See if a word is stretched out, or sung on one note or on several. Each of these instances are clues from the lyricist of the importance of that word and what she or he would like you to do with it. Become a detective and uncover the hidden messages of the song.

Look at the song "Blowing in the Wind." Notice how the notes rise and fall as if they were actually being thrown around in a gust of wind. That is superb composing, where how you are singing is literally what you are singing about. Just knowing that will help evoke that picture when you sing it.

Don't forget to examine the punctuation. First of all it is a great indicator of where to take a breath. A period usually means just that, take a breath. A comma gives you a chance for a quick catch breath. Also note where the commas come in. Are there many in a row? Or really long sentences with no end in sight? That gives you a good sense of how to approach your song.

When I was studying in England, I was shown another way to look at commas in Shakespeare's *Romeo and Juliet*. It was pointed out that Juliet's nurse had tons of commas after every few words, while Juliet would run on for quite some time without end. This showed so many differences between them. That Juliet was youthful, exuberant and unstoppable. That the nurse was older, probably in less good health and cautious. All of this from commas! So let the punctuation tell you a story that you can then interpret for everyone else. On the other hand, don't be reined in by them, if you suddenly get inspired to run two sentences together or feel that a comma or pause belongs where it is not presently written, by all means add that flavor to your song. Sometimes the most delicious change in a song that is well known comes from a singer varying the punctuation. The audience may know full well what the next word is, but you can tease them by stalling before getting there.

It's also exciting to syncopate and add new rhythms that speak to you. Taking an up tempo and turning it into a ballad is effective. I also am a big champion of mixing up the sexes. If there is a song that is usually sung by the opposite sex, switch the him to her or the she to he and go for it! Or leave the lyrics exactly as they are and keep everyone guessing.

This is a good time to make friends with incredible musicians who could re-orchestrate a song just for you. I have had the amazing privilege and pleasure of people creating incredible pieces of music specifically to fit my voice. It is an absolutely magical experience.

GETTING THE WORDS INTO YOUR MOUTH

Americans are not really known for over-enunciation or great elocution. When we speak we tend to punch notes on the same tone for emphasis "I have to go to the bathroom." Not exactly melodious. As opposed to the Brits who proclaim their needs by moving up and down the scale. "I have to go to the loo." Their language is automatically more sing songy. So I use some of the acting work I learned while studying in England to add more pizzazz to singing.

One of my favorites is literally chewing the words. By overdoing the movement needed to pronounce the lyrics, your muscle memory becomes much stronger. The mere mechanics of getting the consonants and vowels into the mouth this way causes them to become second nature to you. So just to remain somewhat patriotic (and utterly ironic) let's play with the Bruce Springsteen song, "Born in the USA." Start with that "B." Really pop it, let it explode from your lips. This tends to get the party started. The rest of the letters in that word are quite a mouthful. Actually there are three more mouth movements to run through. Quite a lot going on for such a quick monosyllabic word. This tells us how to start this song. It is an explosion that is very full and very fast. Takes everyone a little by surprise and demands attention. Very different than how one would begin a song that starts with the word "Why." That word is created at the front of the mouth with pursed lips and then the jaw is simply dropped. Very soft and forward, almost like a whisper. It seduces the audience into questioning along with the singer.

So do this exercise piece by piece throughout the entire song. I will usually work through each letter in a sentence (as I demonstrated in the "diction" section) and then start stringing the words together bit by bit. So back to Springsteen, the order would go something like this: "Born, Born in, Born in the, Born in the USA." Your mouth may get tired. It's quite a workout. Make sure you do lips rolls and mouth chewing to keep agile. Use your hands to give gentle massages around the cheeks and jaw so that you can remain limber.

After working through the whole song, go back to singing it. It will feel TOTALLY different. You have freed up your muscles and imprinted new physical meanings to the words. This will absolutely be reflected when you sing again.

Another thing to notice is how the placement of the words

in your mouth can literally tell you what is going on in the song. There is a major reason Whitney Houston had such a great hit with "I Will Always Love You." Try using the above technique with those words. Notice how much tongue action is happening? And I mean that in every sense of the word. The song is really one big make out session! Doesn't that make it much more fun to sing and way more fun to listen to?

Also pay attention to when your hands move in a song. They usually want to emphasize words that are important to you. Take that as a signal to look at how you want to approach those specific words. The more you open up to the messages your body is giving you, the deeper into the song and its meanings you will be able to go.

## EMOTIONAL EXPRESSION

While you are doing the technical work of getting the sounds and words in your body, you also want to notice how it affects you, emotionally.

This is the perfect time to take all of the different awarenesses, of body, breath, sound, tone, punctuation, etc. and start to weave them together. Your song will already be pretty powerful from all of that work. Attaching the sound to the words should be much easier and the choices of how to sing the song should be coming from a really grounded place.

Now you can make clearer decisions about how to ultimately present your song. Because the song has been living inside you, you will feel how it needs to be sung in certain ways and no other way will satisfy. That is great, the song is starting to become yours. As I said before, the whole point of singing is because there is something that you need to express that can't be contained in mere speech. The passion behind that need is what people respond to without fail. So don't be afraid to let us into your imagination, into your creativity and into your private world. Discover for yourself what that is and then let us in. We will be happy to enter that place with you.

Again, depending on the song and the need, the type of expression will be very different. Are you singing a story song and weaving a tale for us to learn the moral? Are you teasing us seductively and then offering a climactic release? Are you rallying the troops into action with a heroic and inspiring moment? Or are you letting us into a very intimate, painful place enabling us to experience a great catharsis at the end?

Know what you are doing emotionally with your song, and what you want to impart to your audience. By the end of the song, should we be moved? Laughing? Crying? Raising our hands in united protest? Know what you want and then go get it. That is the extraordinary power of singing. Within 3-4 minutes you can have effectively changed the temperature in a room, the racing of a person's pulse, or the course of someone's life. It's potentially that powerful. My parents met a couple who remembered hearing me twenty-three years ago! Not only did they recollect that I sang, they remembered WHAT I sang! Frankly, I didn't even remember performing until they mentioned it. It was a humbling moment. To know that I could be so effective almost a quarter of a century ago that my singing is still moving people today is pretty awesome!

The sign of a true pro is when you can let yourself go but also know when you have gone too far. It's a tricky dance and some people have different tastes when it comes to over the top performing vs. more subtle modes of presentation. So part of it is up to you. And I suggest that you experiment. Try a song with no holds barred, as crazy as you can imagine, then start to rein it in and find the zone that fits you best. Just don't think that louder is necessarily better. Remember, as exciting as it is to get the audience riled up with screams, belting money notes, or majorly loud feedback, sometimes the simple version can be just as effective. I learned that lesson when I listened to Alanis Morisette's unplugged versions of songs from *Jagged Little Pill* done only with guitar. I was used to singing her music at the top of my lungs in the car. It was a revelation to hear the same music done so quietly, differently, beautifully.

## VISUALIZATION & SENSE MEMORY

You ultimately want to own a song. For it to be something that no one can imagine hearing any other way. So here are some deeper, more intimate techniques of attaching yourself to your song. This is more acting craftwork. Sometimes it will be unnecessary for certain types of songs where it is more about the

*Of Course You Can Sing!*

music than the character or the story being told. Nonetheless, it is great to have these tools to use when the song calls for it.

The first thing to do is notice what images the words and the music evoke for you when you think about the song and also when you sing it. If you are singing Gershwin's "Summertime" and you are visualizing a ski lodge, you might want to switch the imagery going on in your head.

What does summertime evoke for you? Are you sitting on a cool shady porch, sipping ice cold lemonade, wiping little trails of sweat off your forehead, letting your body relax to the smell of barbecue, the sound of crickets and the sight of little kids running to the ice cream truck passing by?

Notice I am using descriptive words and all of the senses to conjure this image. The more you can taste that lemonade or feel that lazy, contented body, the more you can give to the lyric. Actually imagine yourself singing from that place. Then just to prove this point, go to that ski lodge. Imagine the freezing crystals on your nose that haven't melted yet as you desperately attempt to warm up by the blazing fire. Feel the prickly tingling in your body as it begins to thaw out. Now try to sing about summertime. A bit different, yes?

Whenever you sing a song without having done this homework, chances are you are putting incorrect or at least un-thought out images into your song. These sense memory exercises can be done in either of two ways. You can go back into your personal memories and find detailed aspects from your own experience. Or you can let your imagination go wild and cook up something very juicy and provocative. The whole point is to get your blood flowing and for these sensual images to move you. So whatever works, I say use it!

Keep in mind, you could have an automatic response to a song or to a lyric. If that is the case, your innate creativity has already done the job for you and you don't have to push it.

This work is also really useful if you are singing something a lot and/or over time. There may come a day or a performance where you are just not feeling what you normally feel in a song or you are upset about a life situation and can't shake it. This is a great opportunity to remind yourself of this sense memory work and allow that make believe session to place you back into the guts of the song. If you are doing a long run of a show or concert, you may also choose to go back inside and make up new visualizations. This keeps the song fresh and will help you uncover parts to the song that may have gotten stale.

It also is useful to imagine someone specific to whom you are singing. Sometimes it's fine to simply sing to the audience in general, but there are many instances, especially in love songs, where picking an actual person makes a huge difference. Imagine singing the same love song to all of the people in your life. Notice how different it is singing to a lover versus a parent. Singing to a child versus an adult. Singing to your favorite plant versus a really cute pet. Singing to Antonio Banderas or Halle Berry versus your dentist or grocer. Each object of your affection causes different interpretations for you. Also where you physically place them makes a big difference. Many singers put them in front of their sightline, usually out towards the audience. That works. Try one where he or she is standing behind you and imagine their arms wrapped around your body as you sing. Hmm…Yummy.

The same is true for songs of anger or sadness or any other emotion that would be really energized by singing it specifically to the person who most annoys you. It can be quite cathartic and the audience ALWAYS feels the specificity even if you never reveal whom it was you were using. Remember this is a private decision. I don't find it useful to ever share who I am singing to which gives me the freedom to really go deep, dark and personal without ever worrying over the ramifications.

I think it is important to make sure you are interested in the song you are singing. I can always tell when a singer has been handed a song that they don't like or was chosen for them. If you have a choice, just change it. I had an adorable little girl come for her first lesson. She had obviously been studying prior to coming to me. I asked her what she would like to work on and she informed me that "Caro Mio Ben" was very good for her vowels. I absolutely agreed with her, and then I let her know that *The Little Mermaid* was also really good for her vowels. I will never forget how big her eyes got and I have to say, the gusto with which she worked on that song was impressive. So, let yourself enjoy your process. If you are someone who likes ancient Celtic music, go to it and in the sacred words of Mama Rose, "Sing out, Louise!" Your enthusiasm will always be catching.

If you are, shall we say lightly, stuck with a song that you are not crazy about, here comes an interesting challenge. Somehow turn it into something you actually look forward to singing. I had just such a dilemma when I was playing the Princess in a production of *Call Me Madam*. This show is chock full of great Irving Berlin tunes, many of which I got to sing. However, for some bizarre reason, the original creators of this show thought it was a good idea to have the Princess enter singing a song called "Dance To The Music of the Ocarina." Oy.

I have to say I was pretty stymied for quite some time. It was just so ridiculous to me. I did not know how in the world to make this song work for the audience let alone for me. I spent quite some time examining what ways I could approach this song without mocking it (a strong temptation at first). And I definitely had to watch my reticence because if I was grimacing through the song, that was not going to telegraph the happy girl this princess is supposed to be. So I thought about all of the things that I love about dancing. About music. How happy I get when people join together in any capacity to create art. I just started replacing my unhappiness with the lyrics with my utter joy in what she was ultimately asking everyone to do. And the more I played with that, the better the song became. Until finally the musical director approached me one day and said, "Michelle, I don't know how you have done it but instead of 'I Hear Singing But There's No One There' or 'It's A Lovely Day Today,' 'Dance to the Music of the Ocarina' is now my most favorite song in the show!" Score!

The other thing to think about is what is your overall intention in singing the song? What are you trying to convey? And then imagine what that could look and feel like. Do you want to be a crumpled exhausted heap by the end of the song? Do you want to feel soaring and triumphant having overcome an extreme obstacle? Do you want to be on the verge of laughing hysterically? Make sure you find the journey that suits your plans. If you want to show triumph, make sure you plant the seeds at the beginning of the song that there is something to triumph over. Are you nervous that what you are singing about can't happen? Add doses of drama to the song. If you pose a question at the beginning, really discover the answer by the end. And bring the audience into the same relief you are feeling by its completion.

Whether I am scoring a character's journey throughout a play or simply a phase of the journey through a song, I want to make sure that the person I am at the end of the song is not the same person I was at the beginning. I am taking the audience and myself on an adventure. And together we share the transformation.

*Of Course You Can Sing!*

# AUDITIONING

## AUDITIONS

It wasn't until I began auditioning other people instead of standing in front of the production team myself, that I fully understood the secret to auditions. THEY WANT YOU TO BE THE ONE!!!!! Please, dear God, after sitting for hours watching person after person not be who they need, they are just dying for that breath of fresh air to walk into the room, blow them away and solve their predicament!

That said, it takes a really smart performer to recognize when they are right for what they are auditioning for and when they are wasting not only the auditioners' time but their own. I am a major proponent of non-traditional casting. I produced and directed an original ballet here in NYC where many of the ballerinas were short or voluptuous. The audience was amazed by the dynamic performances given by every possible shape and size. They were also excited in relating to all of the different ethnicities represented on the stage. So if you feel your talent can outshine prejudice, go for it. If however the casting call is asking for mature Latino men who play trombone and you are a twenty-something red-headed drummer, just don't do it.

If you find you are going on a lot of auditions, keep a journal including all of the info about the audition: what you wore, who you spoke to, what was said, what you sang and how you felt it went. It's incredibly helpful because sometimes there is a time lapse between an audition and a call back and you want to remember everything so that you can build on the momentum you started with that first meeting.

I know this will sound odd to have to say, but please bathe before coming into the room. The auditioner is contemplating spending intimate time with you. That's a sure-fire way to ruin your chances.

## YOUR CALL BACK BAG

It never ceases to amaze me how many people show up for auditions ill prepared. Again, this is something that you have control over, so why throw that to the wind? The following are some basic things you should keep in a bag somewhere in a closet so that if you suddenly get a phone call "could you please come and audition in an hour?" (It's happened to me, and I got the role!) you're not panicked.

## OUTFIT

First of all, have several audition outfits good to go, ironed, clean and periodically make sure they still fit you! Depending on where you live (LA or NY have vastly different styles going on), will dictate the right clothes for you. It doesn't necessarily have to be formal, but do help the auditioners see your body and see that you are comfortable in it. Don't be afraid to create a look that helps you stand out, but I don't always recommend wearing something that might frighten people. Remember, they are not just discerning whether you are talented enough to perform, they also are trying to decide if they want to be around you.

Ladies, make sure your makeup and jewelry doesn't overshadow your face. And guys, if you chose to wear a hat, make sure it doesn't cover your eyes.
Also, many times you will be asked to move or even dance. Have the appropriate shoes and clothes prepared just in case.

## HEADSHOT

Next, you probably need a headshot or at least a recent photo (I once had a kid audition who had obviously just graduated since he gave me his high school photo as a headshot. It was very sweet, but I was concerned that this was his only picture and desperately wanted to give it back to him to return to his mother). It's really simple in this digital age to get a great shot of yourself. And I can't emphasize this enough, do have a photo that when you walk into the room, you resemble. It's really hard to go through hundreds of headshots and pick you out again if you were the one with short spiky blond hair and the photo is of a longhaired brunette. I know of one actress who upped her chances of being cast by buying several beautiful wigs and having different photos for each look. She worked all the time!

## BIO/RÉSUMÉ

Regardless of how much experience you have had, you

*Of Course You Can Sing!*

need some sort of résumé or bio. Even if it is simply to give contact information and vital statistics like height and age range, have something typed up and professional looking. It is usually attached to the back of an 8 x 10 headshot. Also, TELL THE TRUTH. I promise you, you will be caught if you lie. You want to know why? I was visiting a producer friend of mine in Chicago and was looking through some headshots and résumés while waiting for her to get ready to go out. I saw someone who was from New York so naturally I looked to see if I knew any of the places he had worked. Not only did I know the places, I knew he hadn't done the show he said he had, because I was in it!!!!! Can you guess where that person's headshot ended up? You never know who is looking at your résumé. Also, it is always obvious at which level of experience you are coming in with. If you are incredibly talented and lovely at your audition, that will go a long way towards getting you the role over someone else who has worked a lot but is not necessarily as gifted or as nice.

**THE MUSIC**

Then there is the music itself. I can't recommend enough having several pieces always available. The worst feeling is to do a great audition, then have them ask for more and you have to say you don't have any more. Have tons! Be ready to stay in there for as long as it takes to convince them that you are the one. And have diverse choices. I once flipped out a manager I was auditioning for by singing seven songs in a row. Normally that would be unnecessary, but each was so different from the rest, it was like I had put him into a candy store and said he could have everything from chocolate kisses to licorice to lollipops.

Make sure the music is readable and in the right key. If you do anything different than what is written, like a pause, or you hold a note longer than normal, notate it right on your music. Most singers keep their music in a loose-leaf binder. Tape the pages together so that they are easy to turn mid-song. And know the order of your music. Don't waste people's time trying to find a certain song. I always keep a sheet in the front of my binder with the music order so I don't have to think about it.

There are times when you will not be asked to sing a whole song. So count out sixteen bars and even sometimes eight bars of music that show you off and make them want to ask you to continue. Then be ready to continue! I did a rookie mistake way early in my career. I wailed on my 16 bars and when I was asked to continue, I realized I didn't really know the rest of the song very well! Oops.

It is entirely possible that you will be asked to learn new music while you are in the audition room. Don't panic. While it would be incredible if you were a gifted sight-reader and could handle anything that is thrown at you, it is not entirely expected. It is usually understood that people might need a little time to get a song into their head and voice. But don't let nerves cause you any trouble. Practice on your own, seeing how fast you can learn a song. The more you become comfortable with the way you learn, the more you will be able to handle any challenge that comes your way. Feel free to ask them to repeat a section if you are not sure how it goes. Don't be shy about getting help. Again, they want you to be good, so help them help you.

## TOUCH UP

*I recommend having water, mints, tissues, pen and paper, touch up makeup, hairspray, a pitch pipe, a little mirror, and something to read in case you have to wait. And here's a good one: have your passport up to date and ready. I know several people who were offered jobs then lost them because they didn't have a passport and could not get one ready to leave the country within a few days. I did not have that problem so when I got a gig in Germany on a Monday, I was ready to go when they flew me out that Friday.*

### OWNING THE ROOM

Whenever I teach an audition class, I always start with how to enter the room. Remember this is the first impression you are giving. Make every second count. Smiling helps. It's fine to say "hi" before they do. Depending on my mood, I sometimes joke around with the people waiting outside with me so that I enter laughing. Who wouldn't want to work with someone who knows how to have fun? Don't slink in nervously fidgeting and looking slightly nauseous. They know you are probably nervous, but you have already proven you are brave by showing up.

If you are singing a cappella, make sure you know what

*Of Course You Can Sing!*

key you are singing in. Sometimes, if you are nervous, your voice may shoot into a key that you did not intend. I would even recommend getting a little pitch pipe and reminding yourself of your first note just before going into the audition space.

If you are bringing in music, make friends with the accompanist. He or she would love nothing better than to help you get the part. So make sure you both agree on tempo and on where you are starting. Point out any notations you might have made so that they know what to expect. I sometimes ask for my first note just to be sure. Try really hard not to ask them to transpose for you. Or give them music that is impossible to read. Musicians have varied talents. You never know whether this piano player is a brilliant sight-reader but not great with chords. You just don't want an awkward accompaniment to ruin your chances. I have several songs that I love to do, but I never bring them to an audition. They are just too hard and risky to try without rehearsal. If it's that important, I will hire a piano player to come with me so that I am assured we will rock together.

Many times the auditioners will want to speak with you prior to hearing you sing. Or perhaps will want to chat afterwards. Don't let this throw you. Expect it. And sometimes they ask weird questions. Don't let that bother you either. Just be engaging and open and if you feel like it, funny. If you don't want to answer a specific question feel free to deflect it in a fun way. They are trying to get a sense of who you are in a very short amount of time. Practice with friends. Have them interview you. Put together sound bytes about yourself. Quick little fun sentences that show you off. I have worked with the biggest PR firm in the world and we would have sessions of just Q & A to prepare me for television interviews. It really helps to have tried it out loud so that when the time comes, you are at the top of your game.

Because they are trying to glean as much information about you as possible, don't think there aren't little tests going on where you least expect it. I always have one of my trusted friends act as monitor. That is the person who takes your name and gets you ready to go inside. Why do I do this? Because I want to know how you treat people. You may be the nicest person to me in the audition room, but I will find out later that you were rude and obnoxious to your fellow auditionees and haughty to my monitor.

Michelle Cohen

Why would I want to work with you?

When it is time to present your song, feel free to take over the room. If you want to sit, get a chair, if you want to take a moment and breathe before beginning, tell the accompanist that you will give him or her a signal (head nod or hand movement) indicating that you are about to begin. There is nothing better than letting the people in the room know that they can sit back and enjoy themselves, a professional is now in charge.

There are many theories as to whether you should make eye contact with the auditioners or whether to look to the side of them and past them. I would simply say, if you chose to look at them, just notice if it bothers them and then make the adjustment. I just think it is unnerving sometimes, since they are usually taking notes, taking a desperate bite into their sandwich or trying to decide whether you are callback material or not, so I tend to leave them alone.

Here's something you do not want them writing on their notes and I write more times than I can count. DE. Dead Eyes. It's when a singer is standing up there and sound is coming out but there is nobody home. The eyes are the windows of the soul. So show us your soul. It's ok to be nervous; it is not ok to have an out-of-body experience. This is where a lot of the exercises in the rest of this book come in handy. Having someone in your mind or some inner work to connect to will usually help you stay present and the warmth in your eyes will return and remain there throughout your performance.

A lot of times a director or casting director might ask you to try the song again with an adjustment. It is really important that you feel confident enough to drop what you have rehearsed and try something new. They are sometimes merely seeing if you can take direction or they are curious to see a different element of your talent. Here is where you just need to be courageous and positive and try it. Even if it feels terrible. It's just an experiment and odds are if the person asking you to do something is talented, they will help you discover something really new and exciting. Allow yourself the freedom to attempt something even if it feels out of your comfort zone. And again, ask a question if you do not understand what they are asking you to do.

Also, your exit from the room needs to be as impressive as your entrance. Don't storm out, don't be dejected. It is entirely possible that you have NO IDEA how you did. You have NO IDEA what they are really looking for and whether you gave them what they needed. So stay upbeat and positive and make them miss you when you leave. Where did that breath of fresh air go? I want it back!

As for getting a gig or not getting a gig, I can promise you one thing. There is so much more going on than you will ever imagine behind the scenes so DO NOT DO NOT DO NOT DO NOT DO NOT take it personally. I have been made ill sometimes over people whom I thought were the most talented performers I have ever seen who I couldn't hire for reasons that would make your head spin!

# PERFORMING

## KARAOKE

Karaoke singing is a great way to take care of your rock star fantasies and have a super time. Anyone is welcome and there is always someone there to appreciate what you are doing. It is entirely possible that this is where you decide to let yourself go, ignore every rule and just sing however you want. That's ok! However, there are a couple of ways to optimize your karaoke experience if you so choose.

First: decide beforehand whether you are going to be drunk or sober while singing. If you are choosing to be drunk while you sing, just keep in mind you will probably not be in as much control over your sound and your body. It will definitely relax your inhibitions. This might help you do great work, or it might cause you to make sounds and gestures that you don't even realize you are doing. Also, alcohol tends to dry you out, so make sure you drink plenty of water before singing so you don't get parched. And then have a blast. I actually had a student once who knew she was going to be singing at a New Year's Eve party and that she would be drunk, so she practiced while inebriated. (This is a bit extreme and obviously not recommended to anyone under the age of twenty-one).

Second: if you are smoking or in a smoky room, be really conscious of when and how you are breathing. One big inhalation of smoke instead of oxygen can lead to a coughing fit. Smoking in general tends to cut down on the amount of breathing you can accomplish and diminishes your range but I am assuming I am writing to responsible humans who understand the consequences of their choices.

Something I do before I go to an evening of karaoke is try out the songs I am planning to sing. And as I am singing, I listen differently to the recording and to myself than when I usually sing along to a CD. Many times I realize that I don't know the song as well as I thought I did and am relying on the singer to pull me through. Also, I listen closely to the accompaniment since it is what I will be hearing for support when the vocals are dropped and it's me taking the lead. I also imagine the space I will be in, and if I have a pencil or brush or an actual mic handy, I practice holding that as well.

Here is where eye contact is worth its weight in gold. The usual karaoke audience is excited to hear you and if you are good, be near you. So what a thrill for you to single them out and sing a part of the song directly to them. They may smile, start singing along or they may shy away. Either way, you just made their night by noticing them. Don't feel you need to sing to the same person for the entire time. Especially if you are doing a love song. Have many loves in the audience and croon a section of your song to each.

## GROUP SINGING

Singing well with others is a treat. Whether it is as a member of a choir, or Christmas caroling, there is something wonderful about standing amidst others and making music together.

Many people probably had some occasions for group singing as a kid either in a school chorus or in church or on the bus ride to camp. (I had the funny experience of singing on the bus on my way to and from a performing arts camp with a childhood singing partner who consequently grew up to be Mariah Carey)!

There is a distinct difference between having a lead vocal versus singing in a group. It is more important to listen for ways to blend the sound, instead of being so distinctive that you stand out. You may be singing the melody in the group but it is still important to keep that sound in matched tone to the harmony swirling around you unless or until you have a specific solo within the group.

Usually this is where people will be marked off into soprano, alto, tenor, baritone or bass. This is simply to keep a clear delineation about voice type and which notes you will most probably be singing.

Harmony parts are pretty strange on their own, but once blended with the rest of the music it can be exhilarating. Make sure you are listening carefully to which part of the note you are hitting. Harmonizing leaves a lot less room for slightly sharp or slightly flat, so make sure you are hitting the note right in the bulls' eye. I find it easier to learn my harmony part really well before trying to mix it with the other singers. It takes concentration to stay on your part so use your best learning techniques so that you don't get lost in the midst of the music.

It is possible that you may have a hard time hearing your part once everyone else starts singing together. A good remedy during rehearsals is to press one ear closed so that you can hear your sound while listening to others with the still open ear.

Some people have a harder time singing the harmony than the melody. That is fine. They can either work their butts off to learn it or it may be more fun to keep them on the melody and let other more adroit singers sing the more complex parts around them.

## SINGING BACK UP OR DUETS

If you are singing backup for a soloist, it is very important that you do not upstage, out-sing, or outshine that performer. There are a lot of backup singers who are actually more talented than the front singer. Their musical abilities usually have to be spot on to lend the kind of support needed (and many times actual notes that the main singer can't or doesn't sing). So if you want to become phenomenal at singing technically, musically, I suggest paying attention to the background vocals in anything you are listening to or watching. Those are your ace singers by far!

If you are singing a duet, pay attention to your partner when they sing. There is nothing worse than watching someone do their part of the song and then tune out waiting for their turn again. Use that other person's music to inspire you as you reach for the next level of your song. Think of it as a baton toss in a relay race. Give back and forth so that when you sing in harmony, it will be that much more thrilling. See where you two can take a breath together and perhaps syncopate together. It is quite exciting to hear two people seemingly finding a note at the same time as if by magic. Calculate the magic and then make it seem a fortunate turn of events.

The best ways to blend in any group singing is to feel the music being created around you as well as from within. It's an amazing swoosh of energy to join into other people's music and rhythm. Make sure you aren't rushing or dragging a song. Feel that beat in your body and let it remain steady. There are usually natural leaders within a group who either have a gift or tons of experience. They are great people to watch and listen to because many times they are unconsciously keeping everyone in the same song and on the same beat. Discover if you are one of those people and then help everyone else on purpose. Your song is always only as good as the weakest link, so it is in everybody's best interest to help out.

### PERFORMING ON STAGE

Now that you are being influenced by many genres and starting to play with what you want out of your musicianship, here's the other side of the coin to keep in mind. The audience. What do they want? I think it boils down to five basic needs:

*First: Be yourself.*

Ultimately, the whole point of singing is to express who you are, your emotions, your personality, what YOU have to say to the audience. Believe me, you are interesting enough and how you approach a song will be of merit if it is truly coming from you.

*Second: Entertain us.*

Basically, know why you are singing to us. If it is to make us laugh, go for it. If it is to move us, please do so. But if you are up there simply singing for yourself and you forget that there are other people in the room, that's frankly not too many people's idea of a good time. Keep the audience's needs in mind while you are up there. By all means entertain yourself as well; just don't leave the rest of us out.

*Third: Be good.*

Perform when you are ready to perform. Do your homework, be prepared and in great shape with what you are about to present. It's not fair to anyone to watch a performer who doesn't know what he or she is doing and thus can't give his or her best performance.

*Of Course You Can Sing!*

*Fourth: Have fun.*

The more fun you are having, the more that will telegraph to the audience. You can be nervous, that's natural. But if you are not enjoying yourself, take some private time and evaluate what needs to change in order for singing to be the best time you can imagine within your day.

*And finally: Don't apologize.*

NO MATTER WHAT!!!!!!!! It is usually unnecessary, it makes people nervous and it is neither you being yourself, entertaining us, being good or having fun! Just don't do it. If something is going wrong, you may need to ad lib or even halt the show, but make it funny and make it human. I saw the first preview of the Broadway show *Love! Valour! Compassion!* It begins with a beautiful tableau of the entire cast looking out at the audience. As the house lights remained on and no one was moving, it finally became apparent that something was very wrong. Nathan Lane (of *Lion King* and *The Producers* fame) just started talking to the audience, "So, how are you? Anybody seen *Lion King*?" As everyone started laughing, the stage manager came out and whispered to the cast. Nathan Lane then said, "OK, let's make believe this never happened and start again." Which we did and they did. And the show continued with everyone feeling great. So like I said, if something is not going right, don't make it a problem. The audience needs to always feel that they are in safe and confident hands. That's your job to do.

**PRE-SHOW PREP**

There is nothing like performing in front of a live audience. Whether it is an intimate bar or a huge Broadway theatre, the high you receive from performing and getting applause is beyond belief.

Most performers have rituals that they go through for themselves prior to getting on the stage. Some do major warm-ups both vocally and physically. Most do not eat just prior to a performance. Some need to keep really quiet, meditating and getting into a deep mood, while others like to pop around chatting with everyone, pumping up their energy. Some people like to do gratitude circles with the entire cast and crew before beginning a show.

There is an incredible amount of adrenaline that pumps through a performer, especially on an opening night. Artists are preparing physically, mentally, emotionally and spiritually to put themselves in front of an audience. So we are talking about a delicate balancing act for preparation. Please respect your fellow performers and whatever they need to get ready.

## TO MIC OR NOT TO MIC

Something to find out early on is whether you are singing live or with a microphone. If you are singing without one, you need to make sure that the acoustics are such that you can be heard throughout the space. You will definitely need other people to listen for you and do a sound check to make sure you are loud enough. There are not a lot of venues left where microphones are not used. So many people are not trained with big voices to fill up an enormous space. Take extra special care to make sure you are not straining yourself in an effort to be heard. Also find out what level of quiet you can reach while still being audible. I actually love singing live without any electronics assisting me. But I also have a very big voice that can carry easily.

The biggest difference in singing out live versus singing into a microphone is the focus of your sound. When you are singing on your own, you should envision the voice coming out in a V shape. The smallest point is at your mouth and then it spreads out over the listening audience. The exact opposite is true when singing into the microphone. You want to have the largest sound emanating from your mouth and then pinning it into a focused spot into the microphone. This calls for a lot more concentration to make sure the sound doesn't splat out over the mic. Many people do this and it takes away from the precision and clarity of the notes. A great sound engineer can compensate for this, but why take the risk? Also, if you are working in a recording session, the ability to specify where that sound is arriving is a godsend. Think of the microphone as your entire audience and address it accordingly. The great thing about singing with a microphone is that you can really modulate your sound because a good mic will pick up just about anything. The downside to that is a good mic will pick up just about anything, including gasping for breath, over enunciation and any gurgles in your stomach (Yup, I have actually had an empty stomach rumbling over the sound system from a body mic!) So, again accuracy is key here.

Singing with a body mic can take a little getting used to. Most times the mic is a little knob that is attached to your hairline by your forehead or your ear. The wire trails below your shirt, usually down your back into a square transmitter pack that can be attached to a belt around your middle. Sometimes a special holder will be made for your costume. Sometimes it ends up being strapped to your inner thigh! Most of the levels are up to the sound engineer, but do be aware when you are singing with someone not to blast into their forehead (something that happened to me frequently since I was always playing ingénues who get up close and personal with their lovers during songs!)

If you are using a hand held mic (as opposed to the aforementioned body mic), be really conscious of where it is in proximity to your mouth. It is usually unnecessary to eat the microphone, as so many singers are fond of doing. It tends to distort the sound and is pretty gross hygienically. If you are still moved to do so, please be kind and have it sanitized before the next person needs to use it.

It is usually great to keep the microphone a bit under the mouth, closer to the chin. This also helps the audience see your lips moving which is a great visual cue for them. So be very aware. If you have a tendency to keep the mic right in front of you or by your nose, you will want to drop it down a bit.

Holding the microphone is usually a great way to see if a singer is nervous or not. Hands tend to be a telltale sign, and I will always look and see if they are shaking. So, make sure you are in a good, calm place, if you are using a handheld microphone or choose to take it off the stand at some point during your song.

Practice holding the microphone in either hand. It gives you more options if you want to walk around and stand at angles. The other thing to work on, if you are approaching a louder section of the song or your money notes are on the way, you might want to pull the microphone slightly away from you so you don't blast out the system. Practice this so that it is a smooth and automatic transition. It's not really something you want to be thinking about while you are actually performing.

I am personally not a fan of making love to the microphone or to the stand. (Unless you are a hard rocker and it is pretty much expected of you). I would rather see you and your body making music, instead of this phallic looking object acting as a not-so-subtle replacement. Just me. If you don't agree, by all means go ahead and enjoy yourself.

## RECORDING STUDIOS

If you find yourself in a recording studio, welcome to a way cool world! I have been enamored of them since I was a kid, but they do take a little getting used to. You are most usually in a tiny room that is filled with insulation. So you are pretty separate from what is happening and can sometimes feel disconnected. The trick is to turn this into the most wonderful playground for yourself that everyone would rather be inside with you than outside with all of the buttons. Find out if you are more comfortable standing or sitting before getting there, so that you don't make the engineers reset the height of the microphone too many times. And there are sometimes covers over the mics, don't let that throw you. This is where having done all of your homework can really help steady you in a sometimes foreign environment.

Also decide whether you like to have the headphones over both your ears or over only one so that you can listen to yourself live as well as the music accompaniment in your ear. Remember, what you are hearing in the booth is not at all what is being processed in the other room. Try and come out and listen with them so that you are all working from the same aural place.

The nice thing about recording is that mistakes can be erased. But do remember that time and money are usually a bit more of a premium. The more you can nail what is being asked of you in a few takes, the more likely you will be invited back.

## SOUND AND LIGHTS CHECK

If you are on tour, it is very likely there will be a sound check before the show, especially in a new theatre. And possibly a run-through of something that either needs technical attention or just to get everybody's blood flowing. Do find out if the sound people need you to sing at your fullest capacity or whether marking the song is enough. You don't want to shock them with inappropriate sound levels midway through the show.

Getting used to singing under the lights is always fun. Many times there is tape on the stage to help you know where to stand. But it is a good idea to get used to how light hits you so that you yourself know when you are in it or not. There should be a little extra warmth on your face, which implies you are standing literally within the heat of the light. If you don't feel that light hitting you, you are probably not in it. Also follow spots can be blinding so make sure you have had practice with them before the performance. Blackouts are usually quite black in the first few seconds as your eyes get adjusted, but it is rare that there aren't lights from some source that will help you, especially if you need to enter or exit during a blackout. If you still find yourself unnerved or unable to feel where you are, do let your stage manager know so that they can arrange having someone assist you. Nothing worse than falling into the orchestra pit (and yes, it has happened)!

## GETTING YOUR FOOTING ON STAGE

It is entirely possible that what you end up doing on stage is not exactly what you practiced. The body is in a heightened state either from nerves, or the excitement of the experience, let alone, the yearning to do well and the surge of energy from all of those eyes and ears turned on you. Do not be alarmed! For many people it takes quite a few shows to find their footing and feel in their groove. That is why there are previews, or invited dress rehearsals. Do not expect yourself to be totally at peace, calm and Zen the first time out. That takes experience. It's kind of like the first day of school. Within a week you have mastered everything going on and are no longer trying to figure out where your locker is or what is your next class. The same for those first shows. You are still making sure you know the order of songs, proving that you know what you are doing, and working out the little kinks that can only be discovered in front of an audience.

Part of the fun and the fear around performing live is that anything can happen, and usually does. You need to be open and ready and not be in a panic for the "uh-ohs". Assume you know what you are doing and that everything is going to go smoothly. The other thing I strongly advise is to come up with some system for handling mistakes when they happen. There is no way you are going to get through an entire performance without something not going as planned. It could be as little as a slip up of the words or a moment where you stepped out of the light, or it could be a major snafu. But the worst thing a performer can do is obsess over each blunder while the show is still going on. I had a friend who used to simply number the mistake as it happened. He noted it in his brain, and then moved on. He knew that at some point that evening or the next day, he would look at those problems and see if there was any way to make them better the next time. Because his mind knew that they would be taken care of, he could let them go and enjoy the rest of the show. It is really important to stay present and in the moment up on stage, so any way you can assist yourself in doing that is great for everyone involved.

**LONG RUNS**

The other bizarre but cool part about performing more than once is that the audiences are truly different each night. Because of this, they pull out a unique energy from you. Some shows you feel you have them in the palm of your hand and other times you wonder why they are so quiet. Keep in mind that many times audiences are silent because they are listening really hard, or don't want to embarrass themselves with making noise. Don't take it personally if your audience seems, as I like to term it "propped up and painted." Sometimes those are the most enthusiastic people who mob you after the show for your autograph. But do enjoy the different nuances an audience can bring and do not try to repeat something that got a laugh yesterday. That can be deadly and once again takes you out of the present moment where it may not make sense tonight to laugh there.

If you are doing a long run, it is your obligation to keep your performance throughout the run as fresh as when you began. That's where a lot of the exercises we have explored come in handy. Sometimes just changing an intention behind a song or delving deeper into its meaning is just enough to keep you energized on stage for weeks. If you truly feel that you are getting stale, I recommend going back to the basics. Go over the song again as if it is one you have just been handed and see what new aspects you can learn from it and bring to your performance. We should all be so lucky to have some major hit that becomes expected of us anytime we show up in public. It is your job to keep it exciting and interesting to perform.

This also is a great opportunity to play with everyone else who is with you on stage. Even if you are soloing, you probably have musicians around you who would love to let loose and be adventurous. The minute you start feeling bored with your work, that is a good indication that you have done so much internal work, you are finally feeling loose and brave enough to add other people's energy to your world. Talk to your fellow performers and see what ideas they might have to work on together. I used to give my long-running casts little games to play with each other on stage. Nothing that could be detected by the audience, but something that kept them alert. If they had to pass a rubber band around to each other, making sure everyone got hold of it by the end of the show, it kept them on their toes and having a blast while performing for the umpteenth time something they could by now do in their sleep.

It never fails that come the end of a run, you discover things you never thought of before. Maybe it's because you know this experience is coming to a close that you suddenly start looking at the songs differently. It's simply another beautiful aspect of performing as you kiss each note goodbye for the final show and let it all go into musical history.

Something I do all the time and I think is really imperative to add to the performance situation is making this a learning experience for yourself. Before you go on, decide you want to try something that is just for you and has nothing to do with anyone else. Maybe you want to hit a note differently than you have before or wear different underwear and see how that shifts your emotions. Something subtle that doesn't affect the audience or your fellow performers, but completely compelling to keep you tickled inside.

The other thing I do with every performance is pick a secret. It is something that I never discuss with anyone. It is mine alone that I know and I explore during my performance. Everyone is attracted to a mystery. They will sense that you have something going on that they do not know about and it will make you the most attractive person in the room. When I played the role of Lizzie in *Baby*, I noticed how much she sang about her place in the universe. So I decided that she felt she had this secret connection with the sky and stars that was so special she wouldn't even share it with her boyfriend in the play. I literally created an imaginary chord between my belly and the stars. It just heightened my performance and made what I did that much more interesting. I loved how the reviewer said I "sparkled." That just proved to me that my little secret had communicated itself. You can do the same thing with individual songs, too. Just add that hidden flavor to your work, and watch how no one can take his or her eyes off of you.

**BOWING**

A word on bowing. However you do it, formally or simply waving, please take the time to allow the audience to thank you for what you just did. So many performers get embarrassed or just don't know how to take lovely bows, and it tends to undermine the effect of a really good performance.

Also make sure that no matter how you felt a performance went that you give yourself some kind of positive reinforcement. Everyone can always do better or perfect whatever they are currently working on. But your body, mind, heart and spirit could always use encouragement for where you are right now.

Whether it is smiling at yourself in the mirror, writing your own congratulations note, sending yourself flowers or taking your own private little bow...don't ever forget that you deserve accolades and thunderous applause both in the real world and in the hidden recesses of your mind.

# OVERCOMING OBSTACLES

## VOCAL HEALTH

It is imperative that you keep in excellent vocal health no matter what stage of singer you are. As I stated before, if ANYTHING is hurting or uncomfortable, stop immediately and have professionals check you out. Whether that is a doctor or a vocal coach, make sure someone is helping you fix whatever is not happening correctly. It is painstaking and frustrating to recover from vocal fatigue, stress or worse. So try not to go down that route to begin with.

My first vocal teacher used to work with rock and roll artists who needed to be able to scream night after night. It is possible to do that and not hurt yourself with careful placement and awareness. Please be smart. If you are being asked to do extra difficult vocal work, surround yourself with people supporting you keeping in shape and in health.

The best ways to soothe your voice is drinking tons of water. Keeping the voice lubricated is key. Some people like to add lemon to their water, which is fine. Drinking tea is great and Throat Coat ® by Traditional Medicinals ® is especially useful for singers. I like to add honey to my tea; some put lemon in there as well.

Gargling with warm (not hot) water and salt is a great soother for sore throats.

Avoid alcohol and coffee since it tends to dry out the system and obviously avoid smoking when under vocal strain. Many singers stay away from dairy all together as it tends to create phlegm.

I use lozenges all the time. Don't use the ones that can be drying like mint or menthol. My entire cast of Nunsense used to suck on lozenges during the show. I had never tried it before so gave it a go and couldn't understand why everyone was laughing. I finally caught my reflection in a mirror and realized that my face is so small, that the lozenge was very OBVIOUSLY lodged in my cheek as opposed to subtly tucked in like my fellow performers. So I learned to suck on most of it BEFORE the show so that I was not a chipmunk nun for the performance itself.

Steaming the throat is easy and another sure way to assist tired chords. You can take a hot shower or just boil some water and breathe while a towel covers your head and the pot of water, keeping the steam in. Adding Vicks ® Vaporub ® to the water can assist if laryngitis is threatening. It's messy but effective.

Sometimes the only remedy is vocal rest. And that means NO talking or even whispering whatsoever let alone singing. Try not to clear your throat or cough, as that tends to exacerbate the problems.

Hugh Jackman joked that he became an absolute monk during his yearlong run on Broadway in *The Boy From Oz*. But he understood all too well the great toll on his voice if he did not rest in between shows.

## SAVING YOUR VOICE

- *Use Emails, Texting and Instant Messaging instead of the phone*
- *Inform people that you need to keep conversations short and sweet*
- *Rediscover the ancient art of letter-writing*
- *Carry a pad and pen with you to communicate*
- *Be sure to put on your outgoing message that you will not be returning calls for awhile to save your voice and keep your friends*
- *Enroll in a mime class*

When you are recovering from vocal strain and want to get back into the swing of things, take your time before jumping into hard-core singing. This is when humming can come in very handy. It is very gentle and a great way to warm up the system. If you find yourself tiring from simple humming, that is a good indication that you are not quite mended and need more rest.

The more you sing, the stronger your voice will become and you will build up endurance. It's up to you to gauge where you are and how much time you need before you can handle whatever songs you are planning to perform. Be reasonable with yourself.

*Of Course You Can Sing!*

## NERVES

There is not a soul on the planet who doesn't experience a case of the nerves at some point in their career. Part of the life of the performer is learning how to negotiate around this seemingly uncontrollable issue. It is entirely possible.

Keep in mind that sometimes a little bit of nerves is good for you. It gets the blood pumping, your energy up and reminds you of the excitement of being alive and taking chances. It is only when it becomes incapacitating or ruins your intended performance that it can really get in the way.

So first and foremost you need to check in as to what degree of nervousness you are experiencing. If it is simply a matter of some butterflies in the stomach, it may be fine. In fact you can use them to remind yourself that you are about to do something wonderful, and they become your friends. My first memory of nerves was just before I was going on stage in my first performance ever at age six. I was waiting in the wings and suddenly thought "Oh, no! I have a tummy ache!" I had no idea what was actually happening. I was fine the second I got on stage, but ever since then, whenever my stomach flutters a bit, I think of that sweet little girl who took those first steps towards what would become a magical life.

If however, you find yourself shaking and your voice unmanageable, you know you need to deal with what's going on. And if you are getting extreme reactions like nausea, vomiting, dizzy spells or actual fainting, I strongly recommend working through this issue instead of thinking this is what you need to endure every time you want to present your talent to the world.

Obviously doing deep breathing and relaxation exercises are a great help. These are very physical ways to calm your body and emotions. It is also good to do some form of meditation or visualization to put your mind into a more receptive state.

But before you even do that, I urge you to quietly check in with yourself and see if you come up with the source of the nervousness. Have a little discussion with your inner self. What seems to be an overwhelming problem, many times actually stems from just one little thing that has suddenly gotten blown out of proportion. So investigate.

Michelle Cohen

If you are not sure you know what you are doing and are afraid of not doing a great job, that is very different than if you are actually a shy person and being seen or heard is a huge shock to your system. If you are overwhelmed by some really important people who are about to watch and perhaps judge you, that is not the same as if you had some really awful experiences and your psyche is afraid to go through the potential pain again.

All of these are legitimate reasons to be scared. Figure out if one or perhaps all are what are keeping you from feeling terrific. It is really important to know the specifics if you are going to work through them.

Once you have found the source of your issue, then you can slowly assist yourself in feeling confident again. If you are still unsure of your abilities, you may want to practice amongst friends and colleagues who can support your learning stages in a less pressured environment. You don't want to do an important audition or performance without having tried your stuff out first. Because the best way to calm nerves down is repetition. Once you have done your songs over and over, you will find the nerves dissipate and sometimes go away all together. So much is fear of the unknown, so try to help yourself know as much as possible so that you feel comfortable.

If this is a very significant performance to you or people are watching that you are trying to impress, that can derail even a seasoned performer. Adding pressure to an already larger than ordinary life experience can be daunting. Here is where you can add perspective to your thought process. Remind yourself of many other things in your life that are wonderful and are as important if not more so, so that this experience doesn't take on life or death proportions. You may also give yourself a reward to look forward to after the performance is over. Know that you will get this, no matter how well or badly you think you did. Keeping in mind that a CD you have been dying to own is going to be in your possession once you are done, is something else to shoot for and is very attainable. Ultimately though, remember that these are simply people, just like you, with hang ups and times when they get nervous, too. Keep it real.

Being concerned about opinions and judgments is something many people try to overcome in all aspects of their lives. You need a super strong sense of self when you are knowingly putting yourself out there for people to comment on. Many performers refuse to read reviews and stop people before they can give their thoughts on a performance. It is your right to do so, so don't feel badly if that is what you choose. Never forget that there are so many factors that affect a person's experience of your performance that in many cases it is not really about you. If you are singing about being madly, happily in love and someone just broke up with their long term lover and are feeling rather bitter, they may not see all of the lovely work you did. They just may be hurting and want to take it out on you. If you are seeking advice or feedback be very clear of the other person's ability to get past their own stuff and serve your needs.

Do NOT suddenly change a performance radically just because someone spoke to you. Check in with those who were closer to the project and also check in with your own intuition. It can get more nerve wracking to try and change a performance to suit opinions than to just stick to your original choices and know that they will serve in the end.

Strangely enough, performers tend to fall into two categories. The overtly social who love being seen, and lap it up like a cat. And then there are the ones who are incredibly shy and have a hard time making the transition from singing comfortably alone in their room to showing their gift to others. You need to look inside yourself and find the seed of joy that comes from sharing your talents and let that grow. Be honest as to why you want to perform. Is it because you want attention? Is it because you have something you must express and say? Is it because you get to wear really cool outfits? (that was my main reason as a little girl!) It sometimes helps to uncover your wants and needs so that you can address them accordingly. If you are someone who can't stand the roar of a crowd, you may not want to do major road tours and look towards the opportunities of being a session singer instead. There is always a way to perform that best suits your desires. Just explore the possibilities and see what makes you sail out of bed in the morning.

There is also the unfortunate truth that most people have

had unsettling or hurtful experiences at some point in their careers. The challenge becomes how to overcome the memory and fear attached to it happening again.

I am a big proponent of literally asking your body what it needs to feel calm and healed. My sister taught me a great acronym for PAIN. She calls it "Pay Attention Inside Now." Pain is your body's way of grabbing your awareness and getting you to sort through something that is unwell. Just close your eyes, take a deep breath and go to the part of you that doesn't feel right. When I get nervous, my thighs begin to shake! Weird, but convenient because it is not noticeable under my skirt. However, it is a great indicator to me that something is not grounded at all. When I switch all of my attention to my thighs, I can feel how scared they are. Part of me is not ready to stand on my own two feet and present my power to the world. So instead of thinking I am incapable of getting over this nervousness, I now see that I am not feeling quite confident or safe enough to do it. Usually once I source through what is making me feel less than capable, my thighs stop shaking and I am so strong that my performance is even more liberated than it had been before.

A great question to ask yourself when you are nervous is, are you ready? And if the answer comes out no, then why not? What do you need to feel ready and to know that you are? Your hands don't shake when you brush your teeth in the morning. You don't need to psyche yourself into that performance. How do you get to singing in such a way that it is as ease filled as that habitual cleaning in the morning?

## VERY IMPORTANT VISUALIZATION TECHNIQUE

*A technique that many pros are known to use is imagining the best outcome. Go through your entire performance from the entrance to the exit (I actually go through my entire day all the way through to curling up in bed at night as happy as can be). You are sending messages to your body and mind about how you would like this day and event go. The more you practice that, the more likely you will actually manifest that outcome. Your muscle memory will respond to what it knows best. If it is constantly playing with you as you make believe your best outcome, it will start to do it on its own in the real world. Very handy trick. Very powerful.*

Sweating is a big nerve indicator. I have always had a dampness issue that would lessen the further into a run I got, which indicates to me that it was more about how unsure I was than about how hot I was under the lights. I literally had a director send me a note backstage DURING a performance. It said "Stop sweating" which I took to mean: don't sweat it, you're doing fine. But he literally meant: stop glistening. We set up a table backstage with a big powder puff to help me out. But within a week more of performances, I was perfectly dry. So trust that the calmer you are, the more you will simply shine with an inner glow, instead of an outer one.

You being at ease is what pleases others the most. Everyone wants to know they are in safe hands. If yours are shaking badly, it doesn't bode well for anyone. So discover what you need in order to put yourself in a delighted state and the audience will go there with you.

## WHO TOLD YOU, YOU CAN'T?

This is the reason I started teaching. This is the reason I wrote this book. Every time I meet someone, and they inform me quite sadly but firmly that they can't sing, I immediately ask back, who told you that? It is how I begin with new students as well. It is always my first question, because it is never the person themselves who got that idea first. What child doesn't let a song rip at the top of their lungs, sure that everyone is enjoying their music? It is not until someone else, a parent, a relative, a peer, an enemy or a teacher stops him or her that they begin to become self-conscious. And nine times out of ten, I bet most of the time, they were simply inappropriately loud in a public place and were just being told to be quiet – not to silence their musical outlet forever!

So really, whose voice is in your head saying you can't? You don't have to ever confront them or even think about it past this exercise. But, for once hear that voice as something other than your own.

After you have identified whom it is, listen closely to what they are saying. At this point in your life, you have probably digested those words as your own. Well, I want you to get them out of your mind and body once and for all. They are not your words, your sentences, your beliefs or your desire. So why hang on to something old, mildewy and not even yours to begin with? Let it go so that you can make room for new words of encouragement and support. I remind you, OF COURSE YOU CAN SING! So get rid of any lingering doubts that you cannot.

The brilliant thing about life is at any moment you get to re-decide who you want to be. If you wake up on the wrong side of the bed, no one will stop you if you turn around, get in and start all over again. (In fact most people will thank you for the effort to put a more positive spin on your and their day). So, the mere fact that you are reading this book implies that you would love the chance to choose who you are today, and who you are includes being someone who can sing!

What type of singer and how you are received in the world is not the issue at hand here. You need to first and foremost decide inside that you can do it. No matter what anyone has ever said, or what someone will possibly say in the future.

### UNFAIR COMPARISONS

Remember this: if you are comparing yourself to others, you have already lost the game. The beauty about singing is that there is not one single person who is more than anyone else. Because there are so many types of sounds and so many tastes, there will never be "The Best Overall Singer in the World." Like I said at the beginning, Maria Callas can't compete with Patsy Cline, Carly Simon can't compete with Barry White, Elton John can't compete with Bonnie Raitt. They just don't have any basis for comparison.

There is no reason to think in a competitive way. Even if there is a job that you are coveting, there will always be another one later. Or that one can suddenly open up when you least expect it! I once auditioned for a show when it was first being cast that I did not get. But almost a year later, I did get hired as a replacement. I discovered when I got into the show, that the first few months had been medieval torture for everyone involved, and only now was everything settling into a more palatable existence. So where I had been so sad that I did not get the part originally, I was actually saved from a bad experience, and got to play the role at a time when I could relish and enjoy myself! So, trust that

*Of Course You Can Sing!*

if you didn't get a job, or a song or something you wanted, that it is always still possible and if it never happens, there is probably a great reason that is protecting you!

## SING BETTER? OR STARDOM?

Something else to consider as you explore your voice and your capabilities, is whether you simply want to sing better, or whether you want to be a star. Performing ably and performing profoundly are two very alternative visions for yourself and it is important to know the difference. Some people have an innate magnetism that draws attention to them. That does not mean that other people are not talented, in the least. It just means that they are great at what they do but they don't necessarily command heightened attention.

I think it is possible to create an aura around yourself. But I strongly encourage you to create YOUR aura, not an approximation of someone else's. What makes YOU special? What makes people want to hear you and not someone else? It's a sticky, tricky question and not one that is easily answerable. But you know it when you see it. And you know it when you have experienced it. There is a story about Marilyn Monroe, that a friend of hers was walking with her and said, "Do it. Turn it on." Within moments, everyone and their mother was noticing her when just before she had been walking pretty anonymously down the street. Call it charisma, call it star quality. It is something bigger, other and amazing. If you think you've got it, cultivate it.

Now you may be thinking, it's not fair; these people just have a natural gift that I don't have. I will tell you something else that those people might deny, but they would be lying. They WORKED HARD at this "natural gift" to hone it, shape it and make it into what knocks the socks off of people today. They just may not have noticed it as work. It wasn't until I was 20 that I realized there had never been a day in my life where I hadn't sung. And it wasn't just singing. It was hours in front of the piano or my mirror, tape recording sessions, and listening back in order to create something new. I would go through entire albums over and over until I got it right where I wanted it. None of this was assigned homework, it was just a regular part of my playing within the day and I loved every minute of it. I was fascinated by this toy

I had at my disposal and wanted to see what else it could do. No one is stopping you from singing anytime...except you.

Always make sure singing is a joyful act of creativity, expression and noisemaking before anything else. If it becomes too difficult or depressing or formidable, do yourself a favor. Go to the nearest playground, get on the swings and start belting away with the little 5 year old next to you. And make sure that no matter what comes out of your mouths, you both praise each other for a job well done!

*Of Course You Can Sing!*

# NOW WHAT

## THE RIGHT TEACHER FOR YOU

No one is stupid, just differently smart. And everyone has the capacity to learn, it's just a question of finding the right fit. You may be more of a visual learner than an aural one. You may be a quick study and memorize immediately or you may need to take more time in order to get a new idea or sound into your body. No one way makes you a better or worse person; it's just how you are made up.

When you are seeking the outside assistance you need to better hone your skills, it is yours to choose how you want that experience to go. Many people have stayed in teaching relationships way longer than they should have, thinking that was the only option. Not true. There are so many ways to learn, there are so many methods being taught, so it is up to you to get smart about what serves you and what doesn't interest you in the least.

First, you need to decide if you want a singing teacher who solely concentrates on technique or someone who is also able to coach your performance. Not everyone has these skills evenly so think about what you want. Also, there are a myriad of ways to approach the technique of singing and you need to know that no one method is THE method. It's just what has worked for that teacher. If it is not right for you, go elsewhere.

Next, determine in what kind of environment you like to learn. There are private lessons, which usually consists of you and a teacher alone with a piano, paying specific attention to your needs alone. There are also group classes and workshops that could be very successful if you learn from watching others discover their voice.

The frequency with which you study is something to consider. In school environments it can be every day, in private practice it is usually once a week. And then there are of course pocket books to consider. If you cannot afford to go to someone on a regular basis, there are solutions. Find a teacher or coach who will set up a warm up and vocal exercise routine that you can then record and practice on your own. This should happen anyway but if you alert the teacher to your specific needs, they can cater the lesson to a more spread out regimen.

It is entirely possible to go to a teacher simply for coaching for a specific audition or role. One of my students was making her debut on Broadway, and we spent the lessons concentrating on her music for the show and how she could best sing it. We never worked on other aspects of her voice or on additional music.

Also be really clear with yourself what kind of voice you want to be developing. As I said before, I had many teachers who wanted me to work on my operatic sound but since I knew in my heart that it did not interest me and that it would not serve my need to sing Beatles songs, I politely declined, and we worked on my pop sound instead. Ask for what you want out of your lesson and make sure you receive it.

Think through how you like to work and how you thrive. Then seek a teacher who can cater to those needs. I used to warn people that they would be laughing through most of their lessons with me. I like the upbeat, positive vibe, but also, I know that laughing means they are breathing deeper, receiving positive reinforcement for their work, lifting their cheekbones and dropping their jaw. (There is always method to my madness). I have had only one person in my entire teaching career that chose not to return after our first meeting. He was so surprised by how much fun he was having that he couldn't register he was actually learning something. He made a really profound leap vocally which was at odds with his belief system that you can only achieve that kind of shift through serious hard work and pain. I could tell that my approach was off-putting to him and knew that we were not a match.

Feel free to interview your teacher and get to know them. And let them get to know you. They are there to help you and the more you open up and allow your dreams, desires and needs to be heard, the more this person can serve you. The best way to know if things are clicking with your teacher is if you find that your voice is changing for the better and you are getting more confident and stronger in your sound, approach and presentation.

# A LITTLE HINT

*A little hint that took me awhile to put into practice. Voice lessons are where you should feel free to take chances and to potentially fail and fail big. When I first started, (I was only 13) I mistakenly thought I needed to be brilliant every time. This made me tense and I obviously was not making the kind of strides I could have been making by boldly experimenting. So presuming you feel you are in a safe and supportive environment, let yourself go. Let yourself be bad. That's the only way you are going to know of what you are capable. I have been known to walk into a rehearsal room and announce that no one should panic, but I plan to be awful today just so I can see what else I had to give. This puts everybody else at ease (no one is suddenly wondering why in the world they hired me) and it gives me full license to be messy and ungraceful without fear of consequences. Start this habit in lessons. It's a great one.*

## INSTINCTS

More than any other form of communication, Music seems to me to be the universal language. It is why so many yearn to sing. You can make an impression on such a huge, diverse amount of people. How exciting is that? There is something about tapping into the energy of rhythm, sound and movement that ensures attention, connection and release. Getting calls on your birthday wishing you a great day is just not the same as everyone joining in unison to sing you "Happy Birthday." Songs that were sung to you in childhood, be they lullabies, hymnals or nameless tunes crooned into your baby ear, leave such indelible imprints. The ability to do that for others is unlike any other gift I know. To put your voice into someone else's head is pretty astonishing. So trust that there is no way in the world you were placed here and not given the chance to do that.

Listen to the music that fills your heart, that makes you feel deeply, that gives you physical sensations of spine tingles or goose bumps. This is someone's musical soul reaching out to give yours a hug. Discover which music you have the ability to do that with and share it right back with the world.

One of the main reasons to learn diaphragmatic breathing is that it literally connects you to your gut. To the area of your body that houses genuine emotion and instinctual feedback. The more you allow what is happening down there to surge up, forward and out of your mouth, the more extraordinary a singer you will become. So let your feelings and spirit get intertwined with the breath. Let it ride up through your body, attach itself to your well-placed sound and without any shame, embarrassment or fear, know that such a deep and profound sentiment will be received as such.

The more you let yourself go and allow the mechanisms that you have worked so hard to develop take over, the better time you will have. Ultimately, you are a vessel for the sound and the mood. You are literally an instrument for change, for entertainment and for moving exchange. Allow the expression inside of you to be let out. Know that you have done your homework, that you are worthy and that you are right to take up the space you inhabit. Then let the world hear you.

Take a deep breath, hear your inner voice in all its glory, open your mouth and share it with us. We can't wait to hear what you have to sing!

*The End*

*Of Course You Can Sing!*

# ABOUT THE AUTHOR

Michelle Cohen is a hugely imaginative producer, actress, singer, writer, director and coach who connects her diverse talents using a fully toned funny bone. Dedicated to empowerment, her work focuses on ways to help the human spirit laugh, sing and soar.

No stranger to success, Michelle and her many projects have been featured on CNN, Good Morning America, MTV, NPR's *All Things Considered*, and in *People Magazine*, *Entertainment Weekly*, *Maxim*, *FHM*, the *Chicago Tribune* and the *Washington Post*.

She produced the off-Broadway mega-hit, *Schoolhouse Rock Live!*, an adaptation of the ABC Emmy Award-winning cartoon. As a filmmaker, Michelle wrote and directed the romantic comedy, "Beyond Belief". Michelle has worked extensively as a vocal coach and served as an adjunct faculty member at several acting schools, including NYU.

Her published books include *Actually, There is Something Under the Bed: A Parent's Guide to Empowering Their Child In the Dark* and *MenOpop, a menopause pop-up and activity book*, both available on amazon.com. *Of Course You Can Sing! Mobile Phone Lessons* is available at: www.everalive.us.

In her career as an intuitive, Michelle has given thousands of private channeled sessions. Her spot on abilities help her clients grow in positive and permanent ways.

A profound believer in the fact that life should be enjoyable as well as fulfilling, Michelle and her projects are constantly on a wild adventure.

To join in the excitement, please visit: www.michellecohenprojects.com.